MW01108281

From a Window: Serenity

John T. Eber, Sr.

MANAGING EDITOR

A publication of

Eber & Wein Publishing

Pennsylvania

Foreword

    As you peruse the pages of this unique collection of poetry, one thing that is easily noticeable is the wide range of styles. For amateur poets, developing your own individual style is important for a number of reasons. First, it conveys to your readers how you define yourself as a poet. Second, knowing what you like and consistently implementing a set of poetic habits and tools will help you grow and flourish as a poet. When an artist—let's say a painter whose practiced medium is oil paints—maintains and fine tunes their own unique style by employing a habitual set of techniques and elements in their work over and over again, piece after piece, the style and texture of their work soon becomes recognizable and the quality continuously improves. The more effort you put into developing a style you are comfortable with and that best carries out your poetic goals, the better your poetry will be. If you're not quite sure yet how you define yourself as a poet, think about the ways in which you define yourself as a person. What aspects of human life do you value? What traits of your own personality do you value? A person who sets boundaries in their life, who is a creature of regiment and who prides themselves on living a life of structure, might be more naturally adept at metrical verse. A person more carefree, capricious, and free-spirited may have a natural inclination towards free-flowing verse. A detail-oriented person might prefer to practice the intricacies of vowel sounds and word play. Certain themes also call for certain stylistic elements.

    Another way of determining what type of style is most appealing to you is by studying the work of your favorite poets. Whatever attracts you to their work is most likely something you'll adopt for your own. Keep in mind as you work to improve your craft, there is no greater teaching tool than the work of an accomplished poet, and it is the mastered style of their work that puts them at such a level in the poetry community. Ultimately, style is important because, like every component of poetry, it demands discipline, and the only way to write good poetry is through discipline.

John Eber Sr.

Wreck-Collections

I can't remember when a stick stopped
presenting itself as a gun.
Maybe between the discovery of girls
and masturbation.
The past hides beneath a hazy layer of intoxication,
and excavation comes with
a squint and a hush.
Because popularity hinges on
various flavors of the truth,
Unfortunately, the temptation to
artificially sweeten our lives with
lies will arise.

I can't remember when my fingers first
held a pen like a trigger—
such a dangerous weapon in
the grasp of an untrained hand,
with an awkward interpretation and
limited understanding of the English language,
clumsily trampling the slight possibility
of eloquence,
merely equal to a break in
the concentration of
a true master of the craft,
holding on to nothing more than
a shameful infatuation with bleeding ink.

Raymond Joseph Elliott
San Jose, CA

The Sweet Smell

The smell of sweet
The heat on my skin
The wind in my hair
The vision of freedom is finally here.

Falling to my happiness
Falling to the sweet
The wind brings me to my feet.

People all around
Busy as they are
People in and out
Do they feel the sweet?
Do they feel the heat?
Do they feel the earth on their feet?

I feel…
I feel the freedom on my feet
I feel the freedom in my body and mind
It's all mine.

Vicky M. Knaus
Citrus Heights, CA

Graffiti

Green like DC shoes, seeps into the cracks
Glides over the concrete, elements combine

Shhhp, Speert
The red like blood, spilled on these streets
Spatters on the wall
A crime scene

Next goes the yellow, so smoothly
Like the sun's light, washing over the dark
The long dark that surrounds me

The grey is gone, the dark ages done
Left is a vision of color

I will no longer be invisible
A pebble in a gravel parking lot
Quiet tragedy easily ignored
Here is my story piece by piece
I am on this wall

Stitch my mouth shut
Put me in a deeper hole
Because I'm already in a prison
I am not satisfied
Destined to be doomed

My *Frankenstein* finished
Like all parents I leave my child
To stand for itself in the world
To be loved or hated, to inspire or anger
But to be noticed

Lindsey K. Holman
Cape Girardeau, MO

Yesterday Is Gone

Yesterday is gone
Yesterday is no longer here
So forget your worst fear
Drinking beer doesn't lessen the fear
Live for the future
And live every day to the finest and fullest extent
Don't worry about what happened in the past, it's gone
You can't change yesterday, it's tomorrow that's coming
So make the most of the future
It's here so work on it and make a better tomorrow
A tomorrow with you and me
When we can forget our struggle and then we can snuggle
The day we realize yesterday is gone and our future is here
Will be the happiest day of forever!
I love you so much
And can't wait for our future to start together forever

Deeda Daley
Wappingers Falls, NY

Early Morn

Early in the morning
when I'm still awake from the night before,
and the street lights are still glowing,
I think of you.
When the birds have begun to chirp,
and I haven't gotten home yet,
thoughts of you fill my head.
With sunrise creeping up,
and my soul is feeling its warmth,
I long to touch you.
To explore you with sight and touch,
to hold you close to my being,
to explore you with loving caresses.
Early in the morning,
when I'm alone, cold, and lost,
I think of you.
How we spent our time together,
how we'll continue to do so.
Early in the morning,
when the sun is up,
and the birds are chirping,
I know my love for you is true.

Bob Barci
Elmont, NY

Determination

It is said one cannot see without light
and one cannot fly to greater heights
than already have been reached
lest the sunshine should be breached
But our greatest fear we must remember
that we are powerful beyond all measure
and shining brightly for all to see
We give others the right to be free
and shine their own light on the Earth
as it basks in glorious bright mirth
Thus no matter what the task at hand
we must all strive to understand
that we need no other light than this
that which in ourselves shines in bliss

Mitchell D. Keim
Menomonee Falls, WI

Joy

Happiness, cheerfulness, gladness, delight,
All these wonderful things are a great sight,
You can tell when someone is acting these out,
Oh, please, it's not one of these to pout.

God made these things for us,
So we should use them for others,
To show them it's not nice to fuss,
Oh, I just love those who are happy.

Though times are tough and joy's so hard to be found,
Why do we have to leave joy in a mound
Or left on the ground?
If gladness is found, why not make a joyful sound?

Lydia C. Melchior
Perryville, MO

Drenched Under a Dark Sedona Sky

Crashing, exploding, thundering drums of
Heaven, completely enveloped in sound.
Zaps of lightning—intense, sharp, dance
across the sky with spontaneity.
Filling the sky, an orchestration of
light and sound.
Listening, watching, mesmerized by the
black sky and white lightning.

The sky comes alive with motion.
A prelude to torrential rain as the
downpour comes fast and hard.
Standing in the midst of rain and more rain,
I am in touch with quiet calm.
Magic sky, music with crescendo and I
am drenched, but don't care.
Water everywhere, more and more *rain*.

Sherron E. Gorka
Garden Grove, CA

Marching in Burma

Should have spoken out when the hammer went down,
And when the law was read that voices be bled.
Should have spoken up when the land was owned,
And the poor were forced to flee their homes.
Should have dissented when our rights were blown,
But it was too late now fascism had grown.
Should have spoken out again,
When the monks were marching,
But I was a coward and hid in the shadows.
And they tortured our brothers for drawing a line.
I should have fought for dear life
When it all came down,
I should have killed them all
When the shots rang out over roaring crowds.
I should have followed my son
Who gave it all and stood his ground.
I should have cut out their guts
When they hung my son.
Those red-eyed ruthless generals,
Right in the center of a city street.
Should have fought for dear life
And done my part to tear out their hearts.
I should have yelled out and cut out their guts
When my son was hung.

Dave C. Metz
Philomath, OR

Nine

Nine as one out of the bay of Neah
Nine out to the Strait of Juan De Fuca
Nine rowing of the tribe of Makah
Nine searching for a cetacean
A sea hunt for these Olympians
They glide through waves slicing
Thirty-six feet of cedar
Canoe for the sea heading
But finding white sails in the sun
Blazing ahead of the wind surging
High prows on twin hulls of fir
Crew holding oars upright a man
Front holding forth his hand
No not hand but a wing
Outstretched his face the likeness
Of Thunderbird, Yimantuwinyai
His face dressed in a bird mask
The ancient mariner of Kixunai
Splendor returned like a king
Pointing to a spout of water
In the strait nine rowed faster
In hot pursuit after the leviathan

Christopher Pett
Rockaway, NJ

The Seagull

Gills Rock is the home of the Seagull
you may count them but you'll never
get a total
Why?
Because when one gets up
another quickly takes his place
And
They all have the same face!

I once respected the Seagull with such might
I wanted to follow his plight
But then suddenly something strange occurred
I was expecting to land at the Sea or the Shore
Instead they took me to the parking lot at K-Mart store

Christine A. Saunoris
Sister Bay, WI

If Only I Could Fly

If I could fly, I would fly so high.
I would go up into the heavens, where there I would cry.
My heart is big, my soul is small but I'm missing my daddy and that is all.
A brave soldier and a wonderful man; why'd God take you out of our hands?
If only you could fight for our freedom once again, God would see that you were a strong, strong man.
If I could fly, I would fly so high I would touch the sky and almost die.
I would follow the bright lights to Heaven for there you'll see a man named John, and boy did he miss me?
I would walk up and take his hand, and only wish to bring him home once again.
He would be free and back with me at our home where there he would see his loving family that was meant to be.

Victoria M. Weiser
Fort Riley, KS

Create, Create, Create

At a meeting of poets that I once attended
Our host said to go out and create, create, create.
To create is to make something out of nothing.
Am I qualified to make something out of nothing?
How do I do that? Where do I begin?
Is there a spark that ignites
from somewhere within?
Or will lightning strike from without,
in an experience that shatters my being
that I must write about?
What is it about me that forces me
to express myself in the written word?
And when I have written something,
my words scream to be heard.
When I write something
it's not for a private journal.
I write—and I hope to write—something
that is eternal.
I write to express a feeling,
an idea, or a moment in time.
By putting my words on paper,
perhaps that thought will forever be mine.

Danny L. Sheldon
Belle, WV

Love Is Forgiveness

Love is to forgive
And to forgive is to love.
Love thy enemy
A command from above.

It is easy to love
A friend so dear.
But your enemy to forgive,
Not so easy, I fear.

This world full of hate
Needs forgiveness and love,
We must strive for this
And love God above.

Mary C. Heiar
Clinton, IA

Winter

Streets are covered
With cold icy-white
Snow falling quickly
Clouding everything in sight

The earth is quiet
The air is cold
A crisp, frigid chill
As the wind blows

Mother Nature is sleeping
Within her white quilt
Soft as cotton
Smooth as silk

No more crowded roads
No laughs or whispers
Nothing is alive
In the dead of winter

Lisa M. Frederick
Hickory, NC

I Confess to Love You, Baby

I have confessed with my mouth
to only love you, baby, throughout
a lifetime.

I have confessed the first day I
laid eyes on you, baby, I knew that you
were the one for me. It was a good
connection between me and you, baby,
I truly confess this to be true.

I have confessed that I truly love
you, baby, more than I have ever loved
any other man throughout my lifetime.

I know I just saw you and the children
a couple weeks ago, but want to be
with you and the children for a lifetime.

I have confessed my heart cries out for your
love when we are apart from each other;
I find love in your eyes—it makes my world
feel good to know
I have someone that can love me back.

I have confessed that you gave me your heart
and I gave you mine;
When we first committed ourselves into this
relationship, it was a sign of love and commitment.

Monique J. Short
Highpoint, NC

Against the Odds

You're notoriously known, there's no arguing with that,
but how can they judge you without having all the facts?

You bring joy to my life when I think there is none.
It warms my heart to see how great you are with my son.

With the world against us how can we stand?
Can we be together? Do we stand a chance?

Rumors are just that; you never know which ones are true,
but I know for a fact I'm only alive when I'm with you.

I've been called foolish and told you're worthless,
but when I look at you, all I see is perfect.

Why can't I see what they see? Am I lying to myself?
Why can't I think about anything else?

When someone asks I simply shrug, but if I'm honest with myself
I'd say I'm in love.

Loren B. Harmon
Frankston, TX

Autumn's Majestic Wings

So they be called—majestic wings,
Those painful impressions of a painting,
Surrounding hearts and thoughts and winds
Who bloom our candle's light holy anointing.

It's always autumn's wings who hurt,
Those wings who cry and die together,
So they will rise again in spring's life court—
The wings of fall, of high and of forever....

Through ages, these wings follow routines
And cycles of fade and of their rebirth....
And each time, they lay their life's curtain
On augmentative, dimensioned masterpieces.

Impressionist colors of autumn and of the Rebirth
Complete the parade of tragic proportions
In galleries of museums where they all fell asleep
And dream of a perfect recall of tomorrow's illusions.

Catalina N. Geornoiu
Chicago, IL

Africa

Africa: the place where life was born.
Africa is where Adam and Eve were formed.
The earth is brown and the trees are green
    and the sun gives strength to all that it sees.
The tree of knowledge is planted there somewhere.
Africa is where God gave Adam and Eve the life of air.
Adam named all the animals and fruit that grows there.
The beginnings of life had to begin in Africa's atmosphere.
God did not call Adam and Eve in the cold
    because the tree of knowledge did not grow in the snow.
A great earthquake separated the land and some of the life
    on Africa settled on different and unknown sands.
When things calmed down and the fear disappeared,
        the land on Africa became split and the seas took some of life
        on Africa everywhere.
Fear changed the skin color but we all have the same minds.
The African language also changed to all different kinds.
We all had to adjust in our new homes in order to survive,
        some had to be saved,
        so in order to stay warm we had to move in caves.
God knows the place where life first began,
I believe everyone on Earth is an African (or part).

James F. Lemar
Philadelphia, PA

19

The Lift

Gone from what is and twice removed
Are you listening?
What if I believe in neither?
Am I a charlatan?
It seems that a life bereft of belief is not a life at all,
but some plain ticking—
where thoughts and being end up unhappily married in the end.
The lift is now heavier than the gape

Michael J. Bernstein
Chicago, IL

Man Is Destroying the World

The world was once a beautiful place to behold
But now all that glitters is not gold
Animals that once roamed this land
Have now disappeared like chocolate in your hand
Where there were once pretty trees and flowers
There are now factories and sky-scraping towers
Now there are polluted rivers and oceans
But no one is making a big commotion
I wish I could see a day
When the world is clean and gay
But nothing I say or do
Can make my wish come true
Man has done his job
All I can do now is sob

Shayla Tolliver
Georgetown, DE

Dear Mother, My Best Friend

Dear Mother, we miss and send you our love.
Even though you are not with us, we know you watch us from up above.
Anytime we called you, you were there
To give us advice and tender love and care.
We want you forever, we had you for so long,
We can't believe you are gone.
You worked so hard, raising us all, and did so well.
We couldn't thank you enough, dear mother, to tell.
Now that we are grown and have children of our own,
We remembered how you helped us and how we have known.
We raised our children from your way,
Even though you are not with us, you are in our hearts every day.
You are a special mother, and you loved us all in your own loving way.

Joy N. Counts
Wesley Chapel, FL

Unconditional Love

Eyes closed full of pain
The confessions of a sad soul lost in love and can't find its way out
Every turn it makes it cuts the hole in her heart deeper and deeper
Constantly allowing these people to hurt her
Her love is unconditional that's why she is blinded by the lies
She has struggled through life, the lies, and hurt
To believe she deserves nothing but the worst
But her day will come when she makes it to the top
looks down at all that have hurt her and says ... *She forgives them*!

Briah E. Noel-Lacks
Plainfield, NJ

Thank You, George

Thank you, George, is what I'll say
No greater price could you have paid

For people of another race
Who never even saw your face

This sacrifice that became your last
You were so young for such a task

To a foreign country
You were sent
So they might from freedom
Benefit

Without regard for your own self
You gave your life
For someone else

Charlotte Neukam
Hanford, CA

the gratitude from love

hate is easy
love takes courage
trust takes time.

honesty believes in truth
kindness is shown through one's smile
a good heart shows you care.

generosity treasures faith
strength carries hope
and happiness is the simple things in life.

being different makes you beautiful
and when life gives you a thousand reasons to cry,
show life a thousand reasons to smile.

Brittany D. Dollison
Costa Mesa, CA

A Love Lost

You've made me smile
You've made me laugh

Now suddenly I'm writing this
on your behalf

You were strong
like the leader of the pack
I'd do anything to have you back

How many times I've cried
How many times I've asked "why"

Your memories live on in my mind
seeing all the loved ones you've left behind

Consolation is impossible
The hurt is unstoppable

I can't fathom a life without you
Oh God, I hope you feel this way too

The shining star in the night sky
resembles the light in your eyes

I long to see your face again
and trade this life of sorrow and sin

Your name is scarred in my skin
I deny my emotion, but it's only pretend

I can barely breathe
there's so much to feel
still I must accept that this is real

I pray that God keeps you safe,
close at hand
undoubtably we will reunite in the end.

Tiffany A. Gresham
Greenwood, FL

State of Being

This is not necessarily sad, only a reflection but true...
Seems as if I'm numb and cold even though it is hot outside,
it's so cold on the inside, and instead of feeling the cool summer
breeze, I get a swift wind of bitter winter coldness.
I don't know exactly what this is but it seems as if I have annulled
a marriage with love and have taken up a close courtship with
neutrality and a nonchalant attitude.
Even when I have something right in front of me
it's as if it is a ghost and I reach out to touch it,
but it's not substantial, it's not real, it's not tangible,
only a figment of my imagination.
I have also taken a trip through time, the past, present,
and I often think of the future, but as I grow daily
it seems as if I have made the choice to leave the past,
live the present, and hope that the future holds all lessons learned, all
of my potential, and me as the best person I can be.
However, I don't know what will become of this courtship
with neutrality, I can only hope that this is only a phase
and just as people get remarried that I too can become one
with love once more...but again, I can only hope.

Lauren M. Collins
Jackson, MS

Vicissitude of Sentience

Shifting eras, time forgotten
Drifting sands, over roads long trodden
Sleeting, stinging, tracks long buried
Seasons clash, blow after strike parried

Untimely change, subconsciously seen
Recorded, rewind, repeat
Permutation, aggravation
Track after tread, keeps the world in motion

To clasp the wind, seasons of change
Grind to a halt, moving abruptly
Stop the flow of time, grasp a single minute
Embrace the now, with selfishness behind

Words exchanged sentences
Falling past the world
Streaming through a continuum cycle
As we grow older

Horizon reaching, stretch beyond the sky
The epoch of an era, as we fight time to loiter
And when requiem is heard
When vision fades, and goes to black

Flying skyward, Heaven bound
Lain to rest, at peace
The soul finds paradise in promise
We'll remember…

Shifting eras, and time forgotten

Nathan R. Miller
Ellsworth AFB, SD

The Product of Inspiration!

Before one can truly find happiness
One must first find his true intention!
When one is forced to survive
Then thou must execute thine task,
Remaining honorable while retaining his respectable character!

When fortune frowns
One cannot become discouraged,
For he trusts in his God
As his protector!
One must not sacrifice inspiration for pleasure,
Until that pleasure becomes inspiration!

Jesse L. Lindey
St. Paul, MN

Blood on the Floor

Don't watch her in the act; it's too dangerous to see.
Your nightmares start to merge.
As the point touches her skin and gets dragged across gently.
The line of blood appears on her pale white wrist and drops to the floor.
With a second look you watch her fall to the ground,
she lifts her chin for you to see the pain in her eyes while the tears
fall down her face.
She intakes a breath and lies alone on the floor soaked in her mistakes.

Alexandra K. Breines
Miller Place, NY

Within

This feeling inside,
it comes and it goes,
trying to be the best you can be,
but you will never be that man,
'cause you can't escape who you are,
or what you have been,
'cause it's all you have ever known,
it comforts you,
it holds you when you are weak,
it gives you the strength to be more,
to be the man you never wanted to be.

Joshua B. Lytle
Kountze, TX

the ending

tear me open, sew me shut,
just another tiny cut.

twist and turn make my heart burn,
as i take away to yearn.

this thing inside, my heart i feel,
as my worst fear becomes too real.

for now you're gone, as i can see,
sorrow's taking over me.

a painless end, i don't deserve,
my place in hell has been reserved.

Brittany A. Cruz
Pleasanton, TX

Embers Remembered

Remember when your glasses caused a great fire
last autumn in the meadow, Emily?
Tossed aside, they slowly magnified the sun
as we made love in the cool, cool breeze.
Remember how I tried to beat flames with my vest
as you scrambled to dress, distressed?
Helpless and worried, the both of us hurried
down the hill to the cool, cool stream.
Remember the sight of the larks taking flight
and the sight of the smoke climbing higher?
As we waded the stream, it seemed like a dream,
this terrible, terrible fire.
And how I am sorry, so very sorry
for your father's meadow, Emily.
And I'm sorry about his finding out,
sorry for his failure to see.
Still wounded and banished,
somehow I manage to love you, still love you, my Emily.
And if you can remember the meadow in fall,
you may still love me.

Joshua M. Baker
Marion, IN

The Sun Will Shine

The sky is hiding
Behind grey lining
Happiness has gone away
Storm is rollin'
Wind is blowin'
The sun won't shine today

The sea is fighting
Beneath the lightning
Thunder rolls on
Leaves are turnin'
Birds aren't chirpin'
The sadness has won

The rain is slowing
Sky is glowing
Golden light filters through
Thunder still rollin'
Wind continues blowin'
The sun has proven true

The storm is not thriving
Sun is now shining
Happiness has come to stay
Leaves are drippin'
Birds are chirpin'
The sun will shine today

Elisha L. Haas
Morgantown, WV

Paint Your Wonders

Paint your wonder out on
paper
And let it fall without
haters.
Once you are done,
Think about it,
And love it.
After look what it has brought you.
Do you like it,
or better yet,
do you love it?
Simple questions
Bring
Simple answers.
This is simple.

Shanice L. Palmer
Royal Palm Beach, FL

Resilience

Her wounds
she wears them proudly
on her face
for everyone to see
Fearlessness and Resilience
Etched into the scars on her face
a picture of the life
she chose to embrace
Her attacker tried to leave
a permanent memory
a mirror image
of horror, evil and tragedy
but when she looks in her mirror
It reflects her bravery
That she faces every day
with courage, strength and dignity
She lives her life with humor
Though she must shed tears
She lives her life with courage
Though she must have fears
And no horror was enough to buy
her entry to a life of silence
Instead she lives her life out loud
Scars a testimony to her resilience

Jenny L. Beck
West End, NC

Heart and Mind

We always tend to overlook so much
The ways we care and the hearts we touch
It's in one's actions where love is shown
We part as we entered this world with a heartbeat alone
Times taken for granted and never prepared
It's tough to look back at the times we've shared
When I stand unaware knowing you're not there
When I look to the skies feeling your stare
In so many ways confused in my days
With a view of you smile in my mind the love never fades
no way to replace what you mean to me
The time bearing sadness and it's clear to see
I'll see you in Heaven and there we can be
Life is full of many sorrows
Understanding the true meaning of here today and gone tomorrow
To live we must die and it's tough to swallow
Our time will come too, so don't live life hollow
It's hard to see and we re sometimes blind
We may have to part in body but we still have heart and mind

Jeff Ricardo
Norcross, GA

Barbara

Where are you Barbara?
"I am here."
Where are you Barbara?
"I am here."
I must find you, love you,
cherish your nearness for
pray tell you never can be too near.
How can I leave you for even a
short distance? O God it seems
so far away
Where are you Barbara?
"I am here, George, I am here."
You sleep and I reach out to you.
I gently touch to feel your warmth.
I gently touch to be near.
I gently squeeze your hand.
"Here I am Barbara. Here…
Here I am."
You once told me, "You are my life."
How… How can a man be so blessed?
A man comes riding up the long hill.
Over the river, past the pine and
along the lake shore,
Ever nearer, closer
To be beside you once more.
To your bedside I rush to get near you,
A gentle caress of your cheek
A soft parting of your hair.
Oh, what a joy!
A slow wonderful kiss,
My companion is beside me
again so near.
Our hands reach out sliding
safely, securely, a firm grasp.
"I am here."

George H. Kennedy
North Turner, ME

In My Heart

I took a chance and let you in, never seeing how all this might end.
With you my heart I did trust, but was me you could not love.
As painful as that was to know, was harder being on this road alone.
But your heart you must trust, Love is put there from God above, and
could not be stolen by a mere taste of lust.
I know my heart is full of love for you and the life I dreamed for us.
But in your heart was but room for one, and I was never the plan,
was the one who held your past. And for that I knew you wondered if
you could ever get back the love you two once had.
So as always I come in last.
But my love for you will always last, because on my heart you have
left a path, where no other man has ever gotten past, so for me you
will forever last.
Even as you make me part of the past.
My heart weeps over its loss and will forever be lost, as well as my
faith in love shall never open its door to be hurt again by love.
For your love was never mine to have, only a dream I longed to have.
So please don't ever take for granted what you are given.
True love is very rare and from God is given.
For me you were a gift..
Just was taken, never given so for that, I ask of you… to be forgiven

Sherry L. McBratney
Mulvane, KS

Many Questions

What to do, where to go?
How to choose, how to gain?
When to give in, when to give up?
Where to look, where to run to?
All questions I ask myself daily.
How to answer them, I am not certain
With a hopeful heart and soul...
Here I go.

Samantha Kay Tolar
Ashford, AL

I Saw a Ladybug Today

I saw a ladybug today and instantly I thought of you
I watched it crawl 5 steps then shiver and stop
The paleness of its shell enhanced the rose's sweet beauty
My eyes close and I remember your red-lipped kisses
It fluttered its wings in an attempt to quickly fly away
But the cruel winter wind stole its words of comfort,
Everything it ever wanted: a perfect world; destiny; to live forever
Hours passed and the sun gave way to the moon
Like the little engine that could, the ladybug fought hard
But the storms of life fought harder with its vicious rain
Bug in hand, I felt the little creature give out
I felt it fade into the night, never finding home
I saw a ladybug today and instantly I thought of our own
And how warm, strong, and vibrant it is; those three famous words

Edikan P. Brown
Worcester, MA

No Fear

The brisk air shows your breath.
A sure sign that fall is here.
Summer has reached its death.
But with this death, there is no fear.
For we know that next year
Summer will live again.

Linda Corey
Winona, MN

Life

Love: Someone who cares about you and will stay with you in great
    and hard times,
Live: You spend every breath you breathe doing something that
    matters to you and others,
Laughter: Laughing at yourself, others and being able to do it out loud,
Peace: When everything is okay and happy when nothing can bother you,
These components are different but the same; they're what makes up
life and the world, this is what we live for,
Love
Live
Laughter
Peace

Hanna K. Kochenko
Rochester, NY

Falling Petals

Falling petals, pushed by the wind.
Settling on the ground beaten down by the rain.
Did anyone notice its beauty? Stomped on and carried away.
Left alone, soul tattooed the petal and took its beauty away.

Abby Johnsen
Vista, CA

Try Breathing Incorrectly for a While

My heart was jumping
my ears getting used to the steady thumping
him close, so very close
I can't get his smell off me
His voice a lovely murmur
whispering hypnotic words
I can't get them out off my head
And truly I don't mind
Every time the sun rises it's a new day
another day to see him
be with him
breathe with him
breathe him all the way in.

Tiffany K. Willard
Cordova, TN

Break Me Down

Everything had been fine until
You came, blinding me in the night
I became mildly psychotic

And I couldn't do anything
Because you were the bee,
Stinging me wherever I went.
And it's bittersweet,
this piece of you and me.

Hoping that I could find the way
Back home, I became afraid of my
Virtual reality

My face began to shatter and hope
Was lost in the quiet storm of my
Misery.

So tear me apart
Leave me to die
I won't mind, my faith has died

I can't come back, all life is dead
Bring me back to life
And break me again, turn me around
And stab me in the back

Unknown identity, please take me away
To the secret place of his heart

So I may rip it out and
Become something new
I want to reach the heavens
And fly away from here
I need to be saved, come and help me

Arialexya L. Pijuan
Jacksonville, FL

Broken

I showed you my love
but that didn't matter
You took it away
and then made it shatter
You have broken my heart
after giving it to you
but that doesn't matter
at least not to you

Anna N. Stock
Geneva, OH

He Who Wears the Crown

Who can make the blind man see?
Only He who wears the crown.
Who can cleanse the sinner's soul?
Only He who wears the crown.
Who can make the sinner weep with joy?
Only He who wears the crown.
Who can bring down kingdoms so strong?
Only He who wears the crown.
Who can carry us when we're weak?
Only He who wears the crown.
Who wears the crown?
Only He.

McKenzie P. Lewis
Wynne, AR

White Cup

A Cup—It stood upon the table
All milky white up to the brim—
I took to drink but was not able,
For lo! 'twas empty, cool, and grim.

"Oh, Cup! I should have let you stand
Alone!" I cried aloud in grief.
For though I held it in my hand
It could provide me no relief.

I then returned it to its place
To stand devoid of Friend or Fill
All stark and white in pale disgrace
And there it calls the thirsty still.

Matthew D. Barber
Bolingbrook, IL

The Last Scream

Horror forecomes the florescent mind
Oncoming laughs cover all undefined
Beyond psychotic hearts breath the immortal saint
Strong words misconstruct becoming faint
My eyes conflict all that have become clear
Leaving my soul to conceal every uncontrollable fear
Why transvert a common torn lie
Into another beat down goodbye
The stains have once more disappeared
For I have reluctantly been known as feared
Echoes of portrayed smiles seal my pain
My heart may still remain under incoherently sane

Linnea R. Privette
Columbia, TN

Carnations or Daisies

Carnations or Daisies? I sat at the dining room table observing the two vases of flowers trying to decide which ones I liked the best. *Carnations or daisies?* Pieces of fresh green fern scattered among the sweet smelling, rigid, round, red petals all clustered together with long green stems snipped at an angle soaking up the water in the clear glass vase. *Carnations?* Multi-stemmed with tear shaped yellow petals opened up to expose the almost gold centered eye with touches of light green. Some looked weepy and others were full of light resting in a large white vase with a pleasant, caring look in their eyes. *Daisies.*

Lana K. Brisendine-Smith
Pittsburg, KS

The Pain

You have a way of turning my world,
From black and white to gray.
Never to know that one day,
You would be everything but gone in a flash of light,
Never to be seen again.
To know the truth but believe the lies,
Not to know you were the one
That made me cry.
As your name rolls off my tongue,
It gently fades into the background.
The pain is like a ghost,
You can feel it's present
But never really see it.
Moving on is always in my mind,
But the fear of rejection always cover it.
Knowing that I will never really
Love someone quite like you,
Wanting to be in your arms again
Always brings me back to you.
But strike without gain,
I can't take the pain.
Finding someone that truly loves me
Is all I want anymore.
As a tear travels down my cheek
I find the strength to stand
And to know that I can be loved again.

Ashley M. Manning
Monroe, LA

August Rain

Gregory Isaacs was right
Just as Vanilla Twilight
Clouds arrive in the sky
I know exactly why

One hundred forty-four
Clouds in the sky
I would blow them all away
They're just too high

I don't know I don't know
I don't know
I don't know I don't know
This rain makes me so.

Rain in August, August rain
Rain in August, please go away

10,000 miles away
Still I want you to stay
My eyes are getting wet
August rains I bet.

Ian R. Livesay
Long Beach, CA

Rest for the Weary

You forgot to trust where the sun belongs
And quit apologizing for the day you slept
Through atom bombs and funeral songs

You forgot to empathize with fear
And quit surrendering to the voices and the vices
That have always made you disappear

You forgot what it feels like to sink your teeth
Into smeared words, cutthroat and steep like a jagged curse
A rhythmic course designed to burst

You forgot how to drain your mind
When the funeral songs were sung just one too many times
And the aftertaste still buzzed
Of a ticking clock, and all that was

Kimberley C. Anderson
Redwood City, CA

Seasons Between Us

In my summer stare, your last leaves have all but disintegrated
And my own have taken flight above the rafters
Built from your branches,
Met the sun in all its splendor,
And returned to ground to keep you company.
With your winter whisper growing weaker,
I sit and watch and wait
For my turn, for my time to arrive.
Meanwhile, I've yet to find any solace this solstice.

Cory B. Young
Melbourne, FL

Feeling Confined

This feeling of weakness,
of confinement,
It strangles me,
barely living from day to day.
Is there relief from this pain?
Is there relief from this suffocation?
Not even the word help
can escape from my lips.
Just a small tear slips down my eyelash tips,
Even with wings, I cannot fly,
Even with fins, I cannot swim,
And I must stay enjailed
in someone else's sin.

Emily G. Eckert
Manchester, CT

Monster

There is hope for sickness
hope for disease
hope for addiction

yet, no hope for me

There is hope
for repentance
hope for reprieve
I hope for attendance

yet,the church won't have me

There is hope
for contentment
even hope for glee
you can hope for commitment

although, never with me

For I am a monster
with insatiable needs
I have devoured most everything

and, still nothing has filled me

Darrell Laurant
Georgetown, TX

There Is a Sentiment Akin to Joy

There is a sentiment akin to joy
known to the leaf
as it is touched by the breeze
and gains thereby a voice
to speak of green to the root
though seldom may the passion
sink so deep
as to persuade the soul
of color
and if it does
by some subtle means
saturate the shadow
such delight can but grieve
the twisted source
cleaving as it must to soil and stone
so establishing a tension
between life and love
that may in some invite despair
while others perceive therein
the origin of beauty

Christopher L. Mason
Middlebury, VT

The Search

Since the beginning of time,
man has been looking for happiness.
However many of them don't achieve it.
As for myself I have found it,
life is so precious that people take it for granted.
As for me every minute counts.
Often by looking at a man's hands
the incline of them determines the soul he has.
Notice at this moment my hands are empty.
Days will come and days will go.
As I sit here I will wait for you
so I could be happy again.
As I am finishing this I have one more thing to add.
It's okay to hear others,
but when it counts listen to your heart,
it won't steer you wrong, mine didn't.

Melvin Torres
Chicago, IL

Betrayed

I know why this is going down.
Most dreams are shredded away,
Failure pounding at you in sound,
Wondering if this sin is slowly making you decay,
As you sit with bars around
The man in black comes down.

Why did he do this to me?
Why did he make me do this deed?
Why did he beat me?
How was I able to see the lies in the seed?
Why didn't I leave until it was too late?
Because he always said we were lifemates.

Bound together body and soul, yeah right.
It was nothing if not supernatural.
I found out what he was when I found his web site.
My husband was a liar and cheater, naturally.
When I tried to leave, he found and beat me.
That's what he did to me.

As I sit thinking of the past
Bars, laughter, and insults surround me.
Spirit and life leave my body acast
Pain of half-life without him overtake me.
Executioner's ax falls my way
Eyes closed, everything dies away.

Hannah J. Iamkui
Leavenworth, KS

Echoes of the Witness

Witness the windowpane
stained, waynes the rain, drain the dew
trains the tie of the *brain's* force
could that mean
solid brain power
forms , heed, "hears" understanding
beauties silence good/evil
space   balance   one
heavenly, *earthly* spirals
Parallel Universes (more than one)
Come together!
adverb…herbs
Whether, as either of the eye
whether any. No man can tale
this soon to be told, tells this stained ink
Witness the flow as the
glow of this effect heeds the head
Of the causes' effect
Take heed all who walk the talk
Whom all have stalked
Truth has broken its silence
Witness, as this peace is loaded
piece havoc reeks, elemental have cried.
Reapers have sighed
For the call of the one has been made
Witness

Melissa A. Helm
Jonesboro, GA

For Loving Me

Who's to say that lovers are right or wrong
When they disagree and cannot get along?
With love, we learn to be strong.

Who's to say that with love's young rush,
That you can lose one another's passion and
Touch?
With love, we learn to touch with love.

Who's to say that with love inside,
It will hold on each and every day long?
I have learned that inside love's arms is where
I belong.

Who's to say that love is wrong or that it will
Keep you from feeling lost along the way?
With love, I learn that it can go a very long way.

Who's to say that love is nothing more than words
Without any meaning and any feeling?
With love, it becomes real and true when they
Are felt deep down within yourself.

So, with love inside of our hearts and our souls,
The more that I feel it, the more that I never want to lose it,
The more that I want to grow old with you and always be the one
Who's holding onto you, as the more that I feel it inside of
Myself, the more that I really love you, just for loving me.

Denise L. McGowan
Las Vegas, NV

Dreams I Once Dreamed

I have dreams . . . too many to count; some I keep in, some I let out.
When I was a child... I dreamed to grow tall and beautiful.
To have a voice of velvet, and hair luscious and wild; I wanted a
body that curved and a face that broke hearts. I wanted to have
someone love me.
Now looking back at the reflection that stares at me . . .
all I want is to be young and carefree.
When I got older. . . I dreamed for wealth,
I did not care for good friends or health.
I only wanted things, lots of money and gold rings.
All I ever wanted was riches. Now looking back, all I wish for. . . is
forgiveness.
I have dreams; some are faded, some remain,
some are selfish, and some are plain.
But no matter what they are, they are all the same . . .
All my life I dreamed of leaving, of the wind kissing my face, and
the road pulling me farther and farther away . . .
But now looking back, all I wish for . . . is to stay.

Anna D. Calixto
Firth, ID

I wrote this poem one day in my study hall class. I was daydreaming, as I always
do. In this daydream I was alone on a deserted road looking towards the sunset. At
first, I felt at peace, I felt free. But suddenly in this daydream I looked back in the
rearview mirror. When I looked back I saw all I was leaving behind. I saw the faces
of all my loved ones and then I snapped out of my daydream. I picked up a pen,
opened my notebook, and I wrote this poem; a poem about my dreams.

Black Moon

I rise above the weak, but walk beneath the skies of darkness.
With a bloody hand I reach out to you...in hopes you'll return my soul.
Through brimstone and fiery eyes, filled with a distant gaze,
into the eyes that eventually will consume.
The price we pay for a better day...staring at the full black moon.

Kennith L. Ballard
Jonesborough, TN

Only One Love

I close my eyes begin to pray for God to bring you my way.
I hold my head up high waiting for the day your love flies my way.
Only the love from the right man can make my heart mend.
I've been hurt too many times before,
and now only that one love is what I'm waiting for.
I'll be the one you've been dreaming of.
I won't hurt you or let you down
I'll be there for you no matter what.
Anything you need I got for just the one.
In my heart just for you
is the love I have to give
with years to enjoy your dreams coming true.
Only that one true love is all I'm waiting for;
God is the only one that knows how long.

Laura E. Kent
Indianapolis, IN

Life Without You

As I sit here looking out the window I wonder
what life will be like without you.
   Will life continue without you or will it just
stand still for the days ahead?
   When I wake up every morning I sit and hope
that I will never forget your laughter or the
smile you always had upon your face.
   As I sit here wanting to cry I can hear you say,
Hush child, and wipe those tears away, for you
will see me again some day.
   The days we spent together shall never be forgotten
for we will always be together forever within
my heart and mind.
   When I think of those days we shared at church it
is then that I realize that you no longer have to hurt.
   As I think of life without you my mind is not at
ease, until I think of you sitting with the Lord above
who I know will give you eternal love.

Dorothy J. Conklin
Clearfield, PA

Angel Tears

The rain drops fall on my window
Maybe it is true they are angel tears
The love of my life is close
Yet still we are apart
His laughter, his smile, his ups and downs
Are second nature to me
Yet sometimes I can't recall them like I should
After all this time maybe it's the small things
That cause angels to cry

Kathleen Q. Sheetz
Ladson, SC

Heartbroken Flowers Make for a Disastrous Relationship

Petals are ruined, thrown onto the floor.
Gardens are stripped naked. Only left are bruises and a sore.
Break away from this hurt and pain. Gain the trust that made the stain.
Tears run down the face. Make way for that flower; it's such a disgrace.
Never too late to turn back unforgiving time, reverse and make room
    to rewind.
Faith is guessed, questioned at its best.
Time will only tell who in the end will prevail.
Give a rose a chance to blossom.
For now only left are the blossoms of a loss hope.

Neza E. Reyes
Suwanee, GA

Barbie's Mohawk

When I was a little girl I played with Barbies.
my brother did not; instead, he tortured them.

Poor plastic forms of enhanced women, it wasn't your fault.
I braided their long shiny hair.
He cut it off and dyed the stubs with Kool-Aid.

I hosted parties for the non-deformed dolls to attend
he filmed movies with them co-starring Bucket O' Soldiers.
Barbie was melted in the microwave showing effects of the soldier's
bazooka.

Then came Barbie's introduction to Star Wars.
She came back without a head.

Skipper, Barbie, and Teresa are now buried in the backyard.
I don't play with dolls anymore—my brother does not torture them,

but what if I should buy one
for old time's sake?

Lindsey Scharman
Taylorsville, UT

The Darkness

When you feel alone,
chilled to the bone.
Your soul cries out,
you want to shout.
You cannot see, smell, touch.

Evil will feed off fright.
When you are at wit's end,
and your soul has fallen into night.
Helpless, hopeless and lost.

Do not discourage.
It will only cost
all you can give.
And all of your courage.

A ray of light,
a ray of hope.
Love will abound,
even here in this…

The darkness all around.

Justin I. Stroup
Everett, WA

A Beautiful Struggle

This Cycle is nothing but Chaos.
Change, in a pattern of violence
There to absorb the weak and strengthen the strong
There to be the equation of everything
To add up simply, but way too complex to understand
Way too internal for physical.

Naive minds call it pain,
The scared call it their worst fear,
And everyone in between honestly does not understand
And the outcome of them could be anything from a beautiful lie to
    pure beauty.

We cannot escape this, nor was it meant to be escaped
But placed here to be experienced, and then grow from
For the capable of course, not the weak
They were all just for the moment souls,

Or for You!
And this time was marked just for that,
Nothing is a mistake if you don't want it to be,
But the beauty of growth in the sorrow of a struggle.

Jenna M. Cheeves
Brooklyn Park, MD

How Dare Her

How dare her eyes look at me
How dare her eyes stare into my soul
How dare her eyes be faithful
How dare her eyes tell me a love story
How dare her eyes say spend forever with me
How dare her eyes say I love you
Her eyes really dare to say I love you?
Her eyes so hypnotizing
Her eyes so memorized by my touch
She loves me
I love her
Let our hearts be one
My road has just begun
Our love
Our bond
Our connection
Our lives combined
How dare us plan a future to get married
How dare I say marry
How I just don't give a damn
How I thank *God*
How dare our *Love* last forever
How my dreams came true
Just by her looking in my eyes and saying "*I love you*"

Victoria Ornelas
Fresno, CA

Butterflies

Butterflies flap flap
See them in nature's glory
The beauty in you.

Emily E. Edwards
Victor, NY

Because of You

Tear after tear I cry
wishing I could die
Why so hurt I ask myself why
hoping it's just a lie
sick of feeling this way
It won't go away it just stays
Used to be different a long time ago
I was happy and so
now I'm sad all night long
hoping I wasn't wrong
Deep in my soul it wants to come out
but in my heart I wanna pout
one day I'll feel like I used to
and I hope it's because of you.

Erica L. Kestle
Norco, LA

A Name I Like

I did not clean my house today, but this I did instead,
   I took my grandson by the hand and followed where he lead.
I saw the world through his young eyes, the birds, the trees, the sky,
   A blade of grass, a flower red, a worm and a blue butterfly.
I take him in my arms each day, this precious little one,
   And thank God for His loving gift, the joy of my little grandson.
He said, "Grandma," such a little tyke,
   He said, "Grandma," a name that I like,
He said, "Grandma," and then I knew this old world turned suddenly new.

Dixie B. Talbot
Springfield, MO

Okay, So It Did Not Go Well

Okay, so it did not go well.
It could have been worse,
It could have been Hell.

The birds are flying in the sky.
The flowers are still blooming;
they did not die.

The winds are blowing,
and kissing River's face.
Yes, my dear we are still
welcome to God's sweet Grace.

Melva L. Chatman
Gautier, MS

Bug

I saw a little bug trapped
beneath a fallen leaf
and in her eye a tear,
she was alone all by herself
no other bug was near.

She looked at me as if to say
please don't hurt or step on me
for I will do the good Lord's
work if you set me free.

Never was I touched before by
such a little thing to think
that I would end her life
only sorrow could this bring.

How will you do God's good work
so all the world may see.
A little voice replied, make the honey
flow for I'm that kind of bee.

"Here to pollinate for mankind."

Marion M. Guttmann
Pensacola, FL

The Light Cometh

The rhythm is off,
like walking with one shoe off.
A missed step here,
an off balance there.
In need of rest,
A place that stands the test.
Grace and peace,
Until once again,
the symphony rises.

Deborah Billets
Charlotte, NC

Misery

A world of fear
Sea of tears
Road of blood
That is where I live
Fear of love
Tears of pain
Blood of many
That is where I live
Fear, tears, blood
So much more
Than the eye
Can see
That is where I live

Niki N. Webster
Geneva, AL

Love Can't Be Lost

There is a thing that you and I see,
The bottomless pit beyond the sea.
There it sits with your love,
Dragging him down without a look above.
Your heart breaks and time kills,
There you wait for you are much too still.
Perhaps there is an end,
One so sweet,
But is it worth it with this much defeat?
There is a time when it is my turn,
But will I die and forever burn
Just so love can take me again?
I do not know this effortless thing,
Love is a death, one slow and chill.
So I'll wait for that man to return,
For he is my soul,
Without him I'll die.
I do not care for the pain,
I will sit here and wait,
And take the punishment for my true love today.

Andrea G. Fagerman
Keller, TX

Concede

I have all this anger inside of me
It's slowly breaking free
Releasing it into the world so selfishly
You can't understand how I feel emotionally dying
It feels so surreal, somebody help me
I'm suffocating, I cant breathe, I have to leave
I'm gasping for air, somebody let me out of here
I'm trapped in an unknown place, yet seeing familiar faces
How can this be when it's my own dream?
Life isn't what it seems
Where is my fairytale ending?
My heart is slowly mending with pieces still missing
My life is spinning on a spool of thread
Constantly banging my head
To release the negative words I have said.

Alicia Taylor
Medfield, MA

A Vast Magnificence

Life is immense.
If we could see the entire universe all at once it would be overwhelming.
Everything we know and comprehend fits, with room to spare,
in just a tiny, obscure corner of creation.
There is always something new to discover.
There is always another possibility.
There is always more to be seen.
The wonder never ends.
No matter how vast the horizons may seem to be,
we can always expand them further.
Whatever limits we may have known in the past can be transcended.
Whatever borders we have lived within can be crossed.
We'll never run out of room to grow.
There will never be any shortage of ideas to explore or paths to follow.
We have to choose the paths that are right for us
and go well beyond what we dream is possible.
Imagine the possibilities.
Know that even our imaginations fall short
of the magnificence in which we are immersed.
Life is truly a wonder and we have it in the palm of our hands.

Charalotte E. Mosely
Litchfield Park, AZ

Who Will Love Me?

Who will love me?
Will it be the man
that never smiles, who
only holds a mysterious grin?

Who will love me?
Will it be the man
who is selfish and insecure?

Who will love me?
Will it be the man
who is full of anger
and out to get revenge?

Who will love me?
Will it be the man
whose self title
is only meant
to be a friend?

Who will love me?
He will be the man
that loves me from within.
He will be the man
that shares my thoughts
and inner grins.

Meco A. Morris
Fayetteville, AR

Heaven's Rush

Mused to death
With random access
Causing disruption
Unwanted corruption
Horrors of the mind
More beyond this world than the sky
Leave the mind and body
Break into sleep
Offer up your last defense
A dream on the way to death
Lost redemptions
Give reason for our existence
Beginnings and endings of a legend
Are being denied without a cause or effect

Bonnie L. Aleman
Fountain Valley, CA

A Beauty in Disguise

A Beauty in Disguise
I see in my eyes
Camouflaging my soul
While prancing around in this made up role
No thoughts of struggle or the "Blackhole"
A Beauty in Disguise
When I looked into my eyes
Often blinded or didn't recognize
The spark of fire
powered by my innate's desire
Lessons learned guiding me to my own empire
A beauty in disguise
as I looked into my eyes
Until one day to my surprise
My fire was much stronger
And couldn't be hidden any longer
'Cause God opened my eyes
For me to realize
The life I was living was all lies
Created by the Beauty in Disguise

Melody L. Holmes
Sacramento, CA

Caged Bird

From every waking moment
To every time I sleep
There is so much like you and me

From every breath I take to the air I breathe
The thought of you and me
Seems and stays so steadily

The thought of seeing you
Warms my icy heart at the thought of seeing your smiling face
To every aspect of your being bring joy into my life
Oh what a wonderful life for you and I

Though the days have gone by so fast....I realize something that only
A caged bird can tell.
That no matter the song no matter the tune that you sing
There is always one that kills the joy in me and you
So let this cage bird sing and sing... don't let its voice fade
Into the dark abyss in which it came.

'Cause only time and time again...
One smile holds true and that is to see you again.
Let me live this wondering dream...yes, yes it's only a dream.
A dream that I do not want to wake from this cold world
So let this caged bird sing... and sing once again....so happiness can linger
In this one's soul again.
Don't tie me down...don't hold me to the ground...let me live....and
please don't kill me now
For I am you...and you are me...in the world as a caged bird don't you see

Tabetha L. Hilty
Indiana, PA

71

Butterfly

Being free
Using the earth as your playground
Terrified of being caught in little kids' hands
Thoughts of blowing away in the wind send chills down spine
Expressions of their identities printed on their wings
Respecting nature as they fly by
Feeling the wind beneath their wings
Landing on a flower petal
Yielding to taste the sweet leaves thankful to be alive another day

Darian A. Givens
Buffalo, MN

Because of Him

I am who I am,
Never what they want me to be
Because God made me
I am who I am
Taught to walk the right path,
Because God showed me
I am who I am
Feeling happy and free
Because God protects me
I am who I am
Because He is who I am.

Andrea N. Lawson
Canton, MS

Christmas Is a Peaceful State of Mind

Christmas is a peaceful state of mind.
People during the season can be very kind.
It's a time of good cheer
For that time of year.
Christmas is a peaceful state of mind.
Christmas is a special time of year.
Let me make this very clear.
Folks can be very nice
Like fire and ice.
Christmas is a special time of year.
Christmas is a great gift to me.
We bury the hatchet and let the past be.
Don't be a fool.
Let the spirit of Christmas rule.
Christmas is a great gift to me.
Christmas is the birthday of Jesus Christ.
To feel his love is very, very nice.
He died for our sins.
Let the worship begin.
Christmas is the birthday of Jesus Christ.
Christmas is a wonderful time.
It's amazing how I got this to rhyme.
I love poetry.
It healing, you see.
Christmas is a wonderful time.

Sharon L. Suggs
Flint, MI

The Birds Outside My Window

The birds outside my window
They fly around and away
Together
Then circle back
Swirling around in formation
Above the buildings
Outside the land.
I think it's time to go back
To being a bird
Mania
Flying high
Thinking strong
Winding through my sentences
Spewing tortuous thoughts
Always above the grounding
Ground.
Birds dive down
Don't hit the ground
And I may stop
Short
But not for long
For I have wings
The mind is me
A melodious symphony.
But I have no flock
No one by my side
Just my thoughts
Swarming my mind
I fly alone.
I shall fly alone.

Erica M. Loberg
Los Angeles, CA

Silence Magnified

I hear the bookstore humming, the various murmurs I hear
The restocking and un-shelving of books, the soft whisper from the
customer looking for an author,
The soft thud of footsteps approaching, there is an agonizing pound
as a book slips from someone's hands and hits the floor in slow-motion.
There's a soft call of "Tall latte" from the local Starbucks followed
by the screech of a chair being pulled back as they stand for their drink.
I hear the low grumble of a disgruntled employee forced to check
the inventory for a troubling customer.
There's the sound of change falling on the countertop as the store
clerk opens a plastic bag and lets the newly purchased books fall in.
A child runs around asking for a toy train, a soft clinking of keys
as students pull out their pristinely new laptops.
I hear a baby's cry cut through the silence and the fussing of a
mother desperate to calm them down,
The flipping of pages, two friends discussing and recommending
books to each other, a couple looking for the baby books,
The sounds of a Barnes & Noble are varied, and the people within
more so, the sounds of a quiet place magnified by the size and
normality of it.

Maria Salinas
El Paso, TX

Healed by Grace

Healed by Jesus,
I walk in the sand holding his hand.
Healed by Jesus,
He's carried me in darkest of pain,
Healed by Jesus,
The scars, wounds, of thy past no longer holding on to by addiction.
I am free.
Free from self-destruction,
Free from the horrors of the rapes in my past.
Free from the using, drinking, high nights to run from the pain.
Free from brokenness and being alone in my suffering, he's holding me.

I am free.
Healed by the grace and love,
healed by the hands of Jesus I can be okay.
Walk in His light, feel the unending love, the amazing grace.
Carried by our papa in storms and mistakes.
Climb upon His lap when in sorrow or joy.

Amanda J. Sutton
Cameron Park, CA

Little Pieces

The little pieces left behind,
the pieces we bother not to pick up,
the ones we leave and tell ourselves,
the little things we say "forget."
The small pieces that we don't bother to put back,
and in the process we leave a mess.
When we didn't turn back to clean it up,
and those little pieces that we say don't matter,
how ignorant we were to think that way.
Now we look behind and wonder about this mess,
How it got so big.
How the small pieces we left behind,
grew and grew into something else
and now it's out of control,
and you think if only, if only,
you didn't leave it behind.
If only you fix it,
put it all together with some tape and glue.
Because one little piece,
one overlooked, ignored, isolated piece
that you didn't turn back to fix,
and other things got in the way,
the piece you forgot
was the one that mattered the most.

Padmini S. Jagpal
Woodhaven, NY

Tender Tensions of a Moonlit Midnight Embrace

Hands around her pretty neck ,
my skin between her teeth,
leaving ribbons of running red,
with vain prayers to never cease.

Lips so set upon a face
in such a way to blaspheme chaste,
sweet cruelty in this moment
as we atrophy,
juxtaposed in place.

To feel her wrath
is her wandering hands,
a subtle yet sensual tease,
with eyes that pierce the coldest stare
yet inhabit dreams like the midnight breeze.

The blood that falls to stain the sheets
sanguine drops so sickly sweet,
falling from her fingertips
through the humid air past waiting lips.

My eyes set sure upon her bloody breast
to find a place where my head can rest,
as my heart slows down from its ragged race
I reach once more for her embrace.

A single kiss from sparkling lips
to send me to my dream's abyss
to once more feel and see the face
that helped facilitate my fall from grace.

Michael D. Upshaw
Semmes, AL

The First Leaf

Since the first leaf fell to the ground,
To this day it's still amazing.
How summer becomes lost—then found.

The breeze demands its lulling sound,
Hungers many months just waiting.
Since the first leaf fell to the ground.

By freezing storms its warmth is drowned,
It's gone. No longer fading.
How summer becomes lost—then found.

Its warmth and pleasures are unwound,
Winter's cold becomes surrounding
Since the first leaf fell to the ground.

Summer's dreamy haze is spellbound.
Soon the Earth begins boycotting,
How summer becomes lost—then found.

Now Mother Nature has been crowned.
Secrets she is good at keeping.
Since the first leaf fell to the ground,
How summer becomes lost then found.

Julia A. Melnik
Newmanstown, PA

After the Storm

The whisper of wind
Blows through trees.
In the distance a rooster,
Calls out to me.

The early dawn sky
With flashes of light.
A storm's been brewing
Long through the night.

 The storm soon passes
Giving way to the dawn.
The sun peeks out
As the clouds roll on!

I can never imagine
A more peaceful morn,
Than watching a sunrise
After the storm!

Karla K. Haskins
Belton, MO

My Land, My Lady

Oh pain and oppression as it has followed me through this complex yet unsaturated life. Is this an obvious tactic of the devastating one with whom I have yet fallen prey to? Shall I be the one to go forth carrying the wrath of this companion or shall I break the chains of red and go forth into the bright yet beautiful land of you?

If it be by choice then shall I move onward now only to cause eruption in other parts of this land or shall I bide my time and oh so carefully let myself slide through the door without a notice from that pain within?

Only by the choice of my own being I feel that survival of the heart and soul are but the only obvious way to leave this land with all of myself consciously and certainly intact to the point of my own ability for upheaval.

Being nothing more than a new and beautiful land I seek to relinquish the heaviness of the old within me, I seek to now go forward and release the land with which I have known for so long. With great courage and faith within my soul I step forward but one step at a time to know you as I have known no other.

Slowly I feel the warmth of your heart, the depth of your soul, the brightness that abides within the most beautiful parts of you. Oh to feel this new land is to feel as if I have not soared this high outside my realm of unfeeling for not less than a lifetime. My soul has so long ached to be unraveled and my heart to be untied from a virtuous layer of webs from which my old land had entangled them.

The battle within was never a matter of win or lose yet stay or leave an unrevealing matter of the whole being. Unlike my old land I choose to reveal all and save a worthy life by joining this new land in which I do so look forward to exploring to its utmost depths. I hand you my heart as well as my soul to hold so gently yet so passionately with the likes of you. With you I shall stand firmly and do nothing more than shadow you with a love, passion, and integrity never known to your existence.

You are the beginning of my end, my land, my lady.

Janice F. Shepard
Lynchburg, VA

Pain Is What I Know

I know how it feels to cry,
I know how it feels to be abandoned and confused.
Pain is what makes you stronger if you believe you cannot fail,
but what is happiness if pain is all you know?
Living life with a broken heart and breathing with lungs that are
surrounded by emotional barriers,
will I ever leave the ground?
Will people learn how to fly like angles?
Sharks will attack even if you're on shore,
Pain is what I know…

Melinda A. Moses
Hyattsville, MD

Love Isn't Blind Unless You make It Blinding

The right one can be priceless to you
that you would want to cherish that person always and forever
The right one is someone who is like treasure
something that isn't worth finding over again
because you don't know if you find love like this
or if will it ever come back
So cherish her love
Don't fumble her love with a dumb play
like find a sub that can fill that spot that you lost
that can be found again
Show her that she completes
and she's the one you've been looking for all your life

Anthony K. Campbell
Moreno Valley, CA

The Mirage

A mesmerized image was staring at me.
Who was this stranger? Who could this be?

Reaching for him and he simultaneously reaching for me,
Feeling his friendliness as he attempts to discover thee.

From adolescence to maturity,
We coyly aged together in unity.

Daily looking in mine eyes and mine in his,
Exploring my soul and inner feelings.

To no chagrin, the aper I could finally see,
The mirage in the mirror was none other than me.

Gregory K. Tillman
Brookhaven, MS

Friendship Anniversary

It's been a year and four months since we met
That's a date I will never forget
I will always treasure it without any regret
Having you as a friend is great
I hope I will never get you upset
Our friendship has no limits
Being with you is always pleasant
Hey friend, let's hold on tight
To what we got and built
Nothing and nobody can take us apart
Because we are close in mind and close in heart
The time I saw you I felt overwrought
You have never over sight
You got to know me inside out
You looked where others wouldn't
My poetries are my new reflection
So please keep me close to your heart
Every day and every night
Let's always remember our date
It's a date we can never forget
Even though I let you know early or late
Just to remind you the day we met
Our friendship is extant
I'm holding on strong and tight
To what we felt without guilt
So let's live the present and treasure the past

Claudia Walthing
Hanford, CA

Lord, You Are My Strength

Lord you are my strength
when I am weak
you are my voice when I can't speak
you are my eyes when I can't see
Lord you give me the strength to
make it through each and every day
Lord you are wonderful in so many
ways

I have a friend and his name is
Jesus
I can feel his love in everything
I do
yes I can feel his love
in everything I do
Lord you are truly a friend indeed

The Lord's name is the sweetest name
on Earth
Oh! What a loving God, a brother and
a father he is
Praise the Lord amen!
He is so wonderful
so wonderful, so wonderful,
Amen, amen

Karen L. Stephenson
Plains, GA

October

The breath of a wispy willow falls lightly upon the ground
And the ancient husks of Nature's hues lie scattered all around

A North wind blows across the plains never to find a home
And a cold sets in for fall begins; tall trees standing bleak and alone

The warmth of the sun falls distant now and the light is slightly more dim
And cries of laughter and the splash of warm ponds have ended as
autumn begins

Leaves pile high and limbs scratch the sky; trying to rip it asunder
And long passed have gone distant sheets of rain and the deep clap
of summertime thunder

But what's that I hear like clockwork and clear from sea to shining sea?
Now comes the time for October's riposte; it's the playoffs, the TV,
and me!

Jason C. Kelso
O'Fallon, MO

Lonely Road

As I go down a lonely road
I hear nothing not a sound,
I see nothing but me lying on the ground
then I realize this is my life
blank and unreal
I left it stranded and alone

Ivy R. Barnes
Billings, MT

Your Kiss

When I think of your kiss,
the one thing I miss.
The love of my life,
who kept me from strife.
A love like December,
so fond to remember.
So full of play,
As long as the day.
Truly unique, so greatly to speak.
Moments in time,
perfection of rhyme,
poetry sublime.
Love do abide,
please stay by my side.

Marty R. Boone
Fort Mill, SC

Contest

Einstein be damned, the pressure's on
Strapped in, the clock is ticking
Pedal to metal and leaving tread
Peeling through a Random House
Faster forward beyond toward the
Place I need to be and
Wondering who will win.

Circling skidding sliding reversing
Googled road kill left behind,
Spinning past pages creased and scattered
Through potholes gaping or yawning
Windshield splattered with meter and rhyme
Turning Peter Mark where he lies and
Wondering what my rivals do.

Fast upon a yellow wooded place my
Road becomes two diverging
Slowing stopping heart racing
That way or the other and I can't take both
"All the difference" one will make
Revving the four-banger as if I knew and
Wondering where the others went.

Contender or creator idling there
Despite the deadline looming
Wondering which one will finally win
Two roads diverging from within—
Killing the engine, jumping the fence
Trailing him into the trees
Timeless reverence rustling the leaves.

Chris C. Basher
Camden-Wyoming, DE

Stricken

It happened on a holiday,
A sunny September was it,
When a sadness overtook the family,
A child left this world.

A broken family received a shock
On this eventful Labor Day,
A father returns from a trip
To find his son was dead.

A sorrowful mother cries for her loss,
A distraught man weeps and mourns,
Their baby boy left the earth,
Never to be seen again.

The regretful father wished he'd had
More time to be with his son,
But it was not meant to be,
as he fought three tours in the war.

The wife and husband were no more,
Split apart by foolishness,
Separating a man from his child
Even farther than before.

Imagine the regret and sorrow
Felt by this pained man,
To lose his son who had not enough time
To spend in love and adoration.

Victoria L. Emond
Warwick, RI

Go for the Gold

Once every four years, the Olympics are held.
Where nations compete against nations.
They send their best team
who have spent years preparing...
There is much at stake.
In life too, we learn to go on.
To persist, to endure.
The years may take a turn,
we have to learn,
There is more.
Our eyes cannot stay only on Earth.
Heaven above beckons.
The reason we live is much more important
than what we have or have not.
We must go for the gold.

Roma R. Dsilva
Mount Prospect, IL

Terror in Our World

Another year has come and gone on that terrible day of 9-11-01.
That horrible morning which we will never forget.
There will be more terrorists,what you want to bet?
For people all over the world their morning had just began.
Lots of families going to work and some others out just for fun.
Where were you on that horrible day?
No matter where you were it was bad, what else is there to say?
Terror had struck that day for every man, woman, boy and girl.
Young and old probably thinking, what just happened in our world?
War, hatred, racism, terrorism are things every human being should
    not have to worry about as long as they live.
Just stop killing and hating but instead think about something and
    give, give, give.
God Bless America, that land that we love.
We can only count on that special one, and he lives above.

Elinor J. Phillips
Indianapolis, IN

Where I'm From

I am from Barbies
From baby dolls and dress up.
I am from hay tall enough to touch the sky.
I am from the roses,
the "thorn bushes"
where I always got pricked,
running back to my mom.

I am from Hi-Ho-Cherry-O's and Hide-and-Seek,
from Mama and Mommy,
I'm from hiding in the barn
and playing in the creeks,
from "Boys have cooties" to "Work for what you want."
I'm from "Everything has a consequence....
and you decide what you do"
And getting hurt when I was stubborn.

I'm from Do-Do's clan,
melting ice-cream and tasty Kool-Aid.
From playing war
and building forts.

Decorating my room with my favorite things,
Childhood pictures,
night stars,
painted pictures I thought were the best.
I am from the times—
when family is the only thing you will always have—
and knowing they'll never leave me alone.

Abigayle I. Colon
Columbia, KY

You

I can feel you near me,
so nearly I can feel you.
Will you touch me just to stir me,
or will you hide there just to nerve me?
I know that you have passed on,
so the world would have you classed on,
but somehow I still feel you.
You have not quite passed on through.
Do you see me when I'm crying hard,
do you feel me shudder at your memory?
Do you know how tied upon you I am,
like the waves that ebb on out to sea.
Do you look upon my empty eyes,
Do you whisper magic in my head?
Do you know how much I grieve for you,
Do you know I wish I too were dead?
Do you see the clouded sky like I?
Do you smell the rain nearby?
Do you know any of the living,
Or are you suspended in the sky?
I have called your name, your spirit.
I have begged them let you come.
Still I'm here all by myself,
Waiting, I'm the only one.

Jennifer M. Flury
Pendleton, OR

The Souls of Over the Rhine

Cobwebs and spiders fill the corners of the people's lives that can't
stand to hold themselves up
Because of circumstances
Wives die, people drink, they lose their jobs, and lives
Once filled with music and rock and roll

Blood splatters the walls
Of their hearts
Once warm like apple cider
Now filled with oppression
Suppressed by the suburbaners' ideas
Their true greatness gets carried away like seeds of a weed
Not wanted but swirling around your head
Like a cloud of smoke after a California drought

The alleyways are filled with the clutter of my thoughts
Realizing that I need to catch a seed of the sprouting weeds
Swirling around my head
Recognize the oppressed, and raise the suppressed
I may only leave a tiny grain of sand in the litter-filled corridors
But what if it joins with other grains and makes a whole beach
A beach that can give you much more than a paradise

There is a world divided by a valley full of unknown
Stereotypes, questions and guilty feelings that divides you and me
Making me want to give you something, everything I have
Buy a dollar newspaper from you and really give you my life saves
Tell you my life story but I know it doesn't equate to yours
Give you a hug that solves world hunger
I want you to know that every positive step you make

Colleen A. Henry
Mason, OH

Dancing

There are times in life when I am overwhelmed.
My voice overshadowed, overpowered by expectation.
Outside concerns decay my own; I must look inward.

There are so many moments I took for granted.
So many things that I did not or could not appreciate,
feet dangling from chairs or resting on shoulders,
the excitement of riding yellow buses,
the sound of Pop-o-Matic bubbles,
the smell of pristine blue Play-Doh.

But I chose to look forward.
I use words like future without realizing the cost.
Trading innocence for decisions.
Days consist of routine, molded by the hands of others,
regimented by clocks.
Anguished by winding lines that lead nowhere fast,
built on hilltops of devoured dreams.

But windows remind me that possibilities exist.
Devoured dreams make room for new ones.

Gentle snow creates moments where time is meaningless.
Enamored, I spy silent flakes float down to cold earth.
No longer regretting my past or dreading the future.
The five-year-old self amazed at how he turned out.

Swirls of dancing snowflakes, vibrant and unassuming.
Wonderful wisps blanket indecision,
hiding points and jaggedness, hurts and disappointments,
and leaves behind in its wake, unspoiled freedom.

Matthew D. Petrunia
New York, NY

Never Give Up

Never give up because you think you've had enough
Life's challenges are designed to make you tough

Never give up because you think there's no hope
Just ask God for the strength to cope

Never give up because things never seem to go right
There's an expression—At the end of every dark tunnel there's a
light

Never give up because life's problems seem too hard to bear
Things aren't always as bad as they appear

Never give up because you think life isn't good to you
With patience and faith in God, you will always make it through

Never give up because you think life is only full of grief
Life is what you make it—you must have that positive belief

Never give up no matter how hard life seems
Keep a positive attitude, a smile and pursue your dreams

Yulanda Gunther
Sayreville, NJ

I Wish That I Could Tell Him

I wish that I could tell him the way I feel,
The way I love him, there's so much;
I wish that I could tell him how much I care,
How I hope he doesn't get hurt.

Whenever I'm around him,
My emotions are set on fire,
I feel like I'm floating into Heaven,
Where nothing can go wrong.

I wish that I could tell him the fantasies,
The images I dream about him,
I wish that I could tell him the memories,
The way he makes me giggle uncontrollably.

Wherever we are the sparks go flying,
There is nothing holding me back,
He sees the real me,
Not the one I hide from everyone else.

I wish that I could tell him
That I want to stay with him forever,
I wish that I could tell him that I fell for him,
From the moment I first saw him on the sidewalk.

I can't tell him since he has gone away,
And I had to let him go 'cause…
When you love something, let it go,
And if they love you, then they'll come back.

Brittney L. Williams
Mason, OH

Only Then

Deep within the well of being,
Far beyond all rhyme or reason
Lies a spot so securely hidden,
Only God could truly tread.
Simply ignored as non-existent,
Locked away for none to view,
It's the stockpile of understanding,
Life's mistakes and pitfall woes.
Within lies the mortar for all bridges,
For the walls so firmly built.
A carefully guarded ledger carried
To our eternal resting place.
Only through our final breath,
As we lay our head to rest,
Do we trustingly lay it open
Into God's awaiting hands.

Sandra J. Rimmel Tharp
Fort Wayne, IN

And the Sun Continues to Shine

A cold wind
Blowing through town is felt by
All those, living or statuary.

The wind approaches me,
Hairs begin to rise,
Buried memories are released
from the depths of my caverns.

Blood begins
To boil within
My veins, my
Face hot,
Devastated.
Stricken with the guilt of
Re-hashed misconceptions.

The howling of my demons
Clanking together like a never-ending
Chime.

Yet, the clock
Hand turns, the voices mute,
And the Sun, gems high
After such a season.

Manuel A. García
Cranford, NJ

Cup of Sorrows

Lord, please remove the cup of sorrows
     from my heart
My cup overflows—from the tears of my soul.
I'm broken, weak and lost.
My spirit is vexed and seeking solace.
But, no one hears the cry—of the broken soul,
And the moan of the hopeful—goes unanswered.
Lost dreams have dissipated,
     'til there's naught to be gained by living.
My soul must be renewed, if I'm to go forward.
The healing touch of the Master is essential to life.
Without Him, without His touch,
     my soul falls into disarray.
Lord—please empty my cup,
     drain the contents from my soul.
Restore me to Your loving embrace.
Please Lord—empty my cup.

Barbara J. Gradney
Arlington, TX

But You Fly O' Butterfly

But you fly O' Butterfly so how can I do more?
I'd love to spread my wings and fly,
then go from door to door.
Your beauty shines in the light of the sun
like a block of sudden gold.
I'd love to be a butterfly,
and I'd love to do more.

Rooya A. Rahin
Highlands Ranch, CO

The Fall

Beautifully unique and painfully different
Without feeling, without reason
Who needs it?
Falling back into grey
Bathe in the acrid stench of human emotion
Taste the nauseating appeal of sexuality
And what of Pride and Dignity?
An abstract filter to benefit the Ego
Lost in the vanity of Identity
Guidance prescribed by the fellow lost
Shall I carry a chain sweet Saviour?
The lamenting of conception
Like the stealing of Innocence
Forgive me Father for I know what I do. . .

Will R. Brown
Medford, OR

The Hand That Life Deals You

Time is running out
listen to these words that exit my mouth
The truth hurts
sorry but you'll never understand
What goes on in my head
I'm sorry that I wasn't a part of your big plan
I can't be something that I'm not
I can't be your superman
I can't rescue you from yourself
Or your life
But I can lend a shoulder
When you need someone to lean on when you cry
I hope that you make it on your own
I hope that you find that happiness that you've always been chasing
I was just a mistake
An error that you've been trying to erase
I will leave you alone
You'll never ever have to see my face
Never again
Not today and not tomorrow
No more laughs and cries
No more tears and no more sorrow
My life's an open book
But our relationship is like a case that's closed
I'm glad that it's over
It was like a bad hand that I had to fold
Now the truth is out in the open
Now everybody knows...

Frank Castillo
Rosenberg, TX

A Woman and a Man

I notice you standing from afar
You look so beautiful the way that you are
You see me and start walking my way
I think to myself, Oh what a day!
Your long dark hair blowing in the wind
makes me hot all over like warm gin
Your bright eyes and warm smile
calms my soul, and makes this all worthwhile
As you write your phone number, your
hair falls in your face, on the inside
I am going crazy, oh how I want a little taste
I am gazing at your features and I look
like I am in a trance, all the while
my face is flushed and now I am blushing red.
I am sweating like I have hot flashes, you touch my
shoulder and I drop my glasses
I'm shaking all over and my knees are knocking
I feel like the whole world is watching
My head is dizzy and I feel faint, let's meet
again, I just can't wait
As you walk away, I see your backside, you turn
and wave and I can't get my mind right
Oh, what is it that happens between a woman and a man
I don't know, but I want to experience this all over again.

Regina F. Walker
Columbus, OH

In Perpetuum

Christ! I reek of my antecedents,
Long since gone to seed,
With whom I was entombed
Fore I was even sewn.

Not so much a miscarriage, no!
Rather, memories sprung from moldy bones
That gathered into a cadaver all mine own.
Whatever, there was enough of me
To achieve legendry by my scratching and
Screaking within.
I'd listen to visitors without the brick,
But none of them so peery as to pry off the lid.

Yet, did my crying yield for a hereafter of prayer;
Only Time hearkened though, paying respect in
Days, decades and always...
                    Always.

"Always"—the only faith of the grave.
I complied and played dead, 'til at last
The mortar cracked, and moonlight and lilting singing
Revealed the place of the dust's and mine exodus.

Christ! I reek of remembrance;
Of the trespasses of those long ago laid to rest.
Only half of them I am, the other half but epitaphs
By Hyperion's hand erased.
But I am enough to listen to the song,
Among moss and foxfire...
                    Always.

Dennis G. Williamson
Norton, VA

Penthouse Dreams

Penthouse dreams—with roots below,
Through rigors of life—to the top they go.

They bet life's cards—then cheat in play,
They loath the truth—for truth won't pay.

They fold the hand that calls life right,
And play the house that gains them sight,

The sight to see above the poor,
The sight to open every door,

The door to wealth—where power rules,
That penthouse dream that's sought by fools.

They gather all that they can store,
Then barricade at Heaven's door,

There kept from rest and peace of mind,
There trapped where wealth gets left behind.

Just listen friend—I tell you true,
This wealth is not for me and you,

So let the rich control the crowd
With lines and claims—in speeches proud.

Just hold at heart those laws of God,
And spare yourself His chaffing Rod,

The Rod He'll use to set those straight,
Those ones detained at Heaven's gate,

Jesus Christ—King of Kings

Michael A. Farr
Charlton, MA

One Negro Woman's Anthem

I was a *Giant* of a woman among all others
I saw them as "grasshoppers"
Izz a cruel massa
I was feared!
     then
What I had sowed afflicted my status
     and
I fell into a horrible pit for a long season
famished, injured, and alone
     above my head
The beautiful "greenones" continued to live life without
My intimidation, my degradation, and my mental molestation
     when
The hand of God touched their tiny hearts, a collaborative effort
Ensued; which brought me food, bandages for my wounds, and the
word of God for my *Soul* to consume
     My season changed
And I was strong enough to regain—out of that pit I came!
I stand as a *Giant* of a woman again
Do not be afraid "grasshopper dears"
We live in harmony
     and
From time to time, hold hands....

Carol D. Little
Marion, AR

106

Sipping Thicke Through a Straw

What if you need sex therapy?
Something so controlling that each night
it's a struggle to resist
that attention...
those hands...
the technology that allows
for every free thinking phrase to
upchuck into its network.
The smell I used to hate,
the taste that made me gag,
now I anticipate each night
with
pure excitement.
Can I not indulge in what
is natural?
Is what I am doing
Natural?

Stephanie B. Salchli
Frankfort, KY

Love's Destiny

A moment taken
A moment kept
A silence unspoken
A cry left unwept

How could you be a figment of my imagination?
To feel again,
What a tingling sensation

I had not considered it possible
I had not thought it through
The emotion I did not strain for that I found in you

A happy ending I never dreamed could be
Something new written now, my love's destiny

Jeaunae Pearson
Winter Garden, FL

Forever Friends

As if in a Magical Fairy Tale
children played on mystic sands, rimming stones
glistening in the sunlight
across the turquoise waters

One a dark princess of Ebony Rock
from prehistoric times
The other a Golden Sea nymph
A boy child of Regal descent played innocently looking
for pirate treasure
An older child looked official, protecting her territory

Suddenly King Triton Rose, amongst giant furious waves
crashing like a Great God his mighty fork in his hand
like Jason and the Argonauts
Protecting the laughing children

Mars smiled down at their treasured sibling
who would one day start a new beginning for their people
Kraken Rose,
The One Rock where all their people came from, acknowledged
the children, so all the Underworld would be fair and know their
presence

A Dragonstar floated across the shores
and offered a lift to another Kingdom
Sea plankton and sea snails accompanied them
on An Adventure they would never forget,
chronicled by Garnets.

Lorraine H. Mosley
Kissimmee, FL

I was thrilled with the publication of this poem and I want to thank Eber & Wein Publishing for this wonderful opportunity.

The Lonely Soldier

There I am cold and wounded lying in the dirt.
Bullets flying by my head as I cry out I'm hurt.
Nobody listens to my plea; they are all too busy trying to flee.
Lying on the ground scared and alone I feel like nobody cares and
I am on my own. When I joined up I planned to fight,
knowing I'd be battling each day and night.
I have made it this far in the war with just a few more weeks
until we settle the score.
I want to live to see that day so my best
hope now is just lie here and pray.
I don't know why but my eyes really itched,
that's when I saw it a five-foot ditch.
If I wanted to live I would have to crawl only fifty yards out that was all.
My adrenalin was pumping through my veins.
I could feel my emotions going down the drain.
That's when I did it I got up and ran!
I ran to the ditch as fast as I can,
I ran, I ran with all kinds of pride I felt
my fallen brothers running by my side.
It felt like forever but I was finally there,
I dove in the ditch and started to stare.
I started to stare at a medic there!
I asked him in shock to radio help but he didn't speak he just yelped.
I grabbed his phone from his pack and
called in an immediate air strike attack.
I thanked God that they got my call.
They will see a huge flash which will end it all!

Andrew J. Ott
Modesto, CA

I Need You

I see so much beautiful things in your eyes.
When I was with you I felt so much warmness,
when I rested my head on your chest
I was hearing your heart beating and it's as if it was speaking to me.
It was saying that you need me and we need
to be together it needs my heart and love to be whole.

Lucrecia Barragan
Phoenix, AZ

My Wish for Your

I wish you sunshine through your tears
Joy to come through all of your fears
I wish you strength through lonely miles
Someone who will share a smile
I wish you love along the way
a quiet time to kneel and pray
I wish you friends who will be there
to give you comfort and show they care
I wish you freedom your life through
Courage to make your dreams come true
Most of all I wish you hope and peace within
May God bless you with wonderful friends

Kay T. Seymour
Lilburn, GA

The Road to Success

One day I was walking
and just so happened to see
two different paths ahead
in front of me.
I knew right then
there was a choice to be made.
One path was beautiful,
the other of dark shade.
I liked the bright one
much, much more
than the dark one
I had been down before.
So of course,
I did as I pleased
and I know that the beautiful one
has made me succeed.

Savannah R. Jones
Black Oak, AR

I'm fourteen years old and attend Riverside High as a freshman. I love reading and writing poetry, but as much as I love it, I hope for my career to take off in the US Air Force when I get out of school. I guess my inspiration for this poem "Road to Success" was how I want to be successful in my own life and achieve all of my own goals that I have set out for myself. I also hope this poem inspires you to want to be successful in your own future, too.

Black Genesis

Let's go back to the beginning, the start the origin
Let's discuss our rich history and the things that make us whole again
I'm on a roll again and I'm accompanied by friends
My ghetto philosophy will be heard in places like Wisconsin and Oregon
I was born to win, this is Black owned again
I'm taking back what's ours and making it strong again
Having this knowledge means nothing if I don't give it back to you
One of the first human remains was found in Africa
To know our past is to know where we're headed
Does it make it fact because the white man said it?
They are pompous idiots known to be big-headed
Let them tell the story of Black history you can forget it
Their version of our history the truth would be lost
They gained treasures from Black countries but at what cost
Separating black families from each other
Siblings torn apart from father and mother
I'm here to be strong for all of my peers
It takes everything that I have to hold back these tears
Rewrite the Black Bible by starting with *Black Genesis*
I would have more facts but the white man hung all my witnesses
He wants me to tap-dance and smile like it's show biz
You try to demean me so I can go home and take it out on my kids
You wrote the beginning but I'm going to write the ending
Prayers of hope are what I'm sending
I'm asking for redemption, hope and salvation
Lord please allow me to write in the Black Bible the book of
Revelations

Tajiye L. Antwine
Sacramento, CA

Shower of Love

Rivulets of water fell passionate against my wet silky body.
Suddenly my thoughts drifted into you.
As I brushed myself gently I imagined my touch to be that of yours.
Skillfully you combed my needy body into an avalanche of pleasure.
Such a soft, romantic kind of touch.

A touch that one only feels in a moment of true desire.
As the rivulets of water cascade down my body,
I imagined feeling your bareness against my own.
Our wet blazen bodies pressed tightly against one of the other.

My lips craving for yours as the warm water fell tenderly into my face.
I drifted back to a place when I could feel your breath in my face.
As you kiss my mouth with loving passion.

Your saucy way copulating my inner need.
A need to come undone, a need to feel satisfied.
As my thoughts reached into a finale,
my body rejoiced in all its revelry.
Tenderly you touch me rendering me helpless.

There I stood under the sultry water in a trance.
In such a burning fantasy, you neared me.
Sedulously taking me into your loving arms,
as I surrendered into you.

In all my aching need, in all my unquenched thirst,
and in all my craving hunger.
My body shook and crumbled under those rivulets of water.
With you in my thoughts, with you against my body,
and with you in my heart.

Rose M. Rotondo
Newhall, CA

The Pains of Being Great

When greatness falls, it falls on us hard,
And when it comes down we're usually scared.
That is mostly because; it comes as a trial,
And we usually must bear it for quite a long while.
It's usually longer then we think we can bear,
But when we finally look up, we're already there.
Two things to remember are: it is never fate
That put us where we are or made anyone great.
It's your own blood and sweat, that put you in your shoes.
Greatness is work; it's a hard thing to choose.
Second, remember that it's worse to remain.
Harder to remain great, you'll see a good deal of pain.
It's hard to have kids but it's harder to raise them.
It's hard to be made great, but it's harder to please men
For any period of time, you'll see that it's tough.
To remain great is always more rough.

Nicholas K. Doney
Marshfield, WI

Your Love

Like a myth; a legend
Your candid love and affection
Became the focus of my dreams and thoughts; my attention
Moreover making my every burden an elation
Making my judgment lucid and virtuous
Through my words and actions, of my fervor a reflection

Samantha Galvan
San Luis, AZ

My Shelter

One day my mind wasn't right
I slipped into darkness
I took my eyes off the light
Tortured and tormented, yes I was
because I doubted the word of God
I knew that if I died today or tomorrow
My soul would be filled with pain and sorrow
So I started to seek Jesus
Because God sent him to save us
to restore our lost souls and rejoice in our spirits
For when Jesus speaks anything that is unclean can't stand
near him

Alisia L. Hazard
Louisville, KY

The inspiration for this poem came from my mother who is a firm believer in God.
My son Jordan and husband Charles have been a great help to me in my writings.

The Lady

She had a face like edelweiss
Violet eyes and carnation lips
And a smile that bloomed in
The golden rays.
Slim like a butterfly,
Bright like a bee,
With warm, familiar
Buzzing of the lips, between
The teeth.
She hums...
You are my sunshine,
A southern lullaby, whispered
In the breeze.
It floats over sunny wheat,
It passes over the winding dirt road;
It tickles the husks on the ears of corn,
And settles at the tip of her tongue.
It hovers there like sugar.
But her tongue is not sugar; It is a rose,
Blooming behind carnation lips.

Alexandra G. Wimberley
Durham, NC

Every Turn in the Road Requires a Choice

The choices that you made
seemed to break my heart in two,
and I know you thought
I would never forgive you.

For all those times I yelled at you,
and all the fights we've had,
I want you to know you've hurt me,
but now it isn't that bad.

Please don't beg me,
I'm ready to forgive,
and a life without you
is one I'm not willing to live.

And know that I don't hate you,
and know I never will.
I loved you way back then, my dear,
please know I love you still.

Alexa K. Asmus
Lake Stevens, WA

I am honored to appear in this anthology. This is my first real opportunity to have something published and I am so excited! I truly did not think something like this would come out of searching through poetry websites late one night. I was just looking for someone to give me a chance to share my poetry. Thank you for taking the time to read the beauty in newcoming poetry. Thank you to Eber & Wein Publishing for making it possible!

History

Disrespected and arrested by cops,
To a man with a dream, on a mountaintop.

To a woman on a bus, who would boycott,
To sit-ins at Jerry's soda shop.

To picket signs and protest for peace,
To negative force, from fire and police.

Into the Black House, and a vote for change
To the Republicans, who grew hair and fangs

To budget cuts, and workers laid off,
While big wigs go out and play golf.

To peace and honors, to hopes and dreams,
To my fellow peers, who must grow wings.

To a brand new dawning, changing hands,
To "I have a Dream," to "Yes, we can."

Under leadership that's long overdue,
My brown eyes don't have to be blue.

Kevin Wilkins
Baltimore, MD

I Wish

When I'm alone I wish you were with me.
When I see you I wish you would notice me.
When I pass you in the hall I wish you would know how I feel.
When you are with your friends I wish you would leave them to be with me.
When our eyes meet for two seconds I wish you would kiss me.
I know these wishes won't come true.
But my last wish is: I wish I could get over you.

Allysa D. Comp
Spearman, TX

A Tear

It starts at the eye
Then rolls down the cheek
People start to ask why
And you try not to sound weak
Wiped away by the hand
Trying to hide
Like being washed in the sand
Swept up in the tide
You say its not out of fear
But it's so obvious and clear
I see it again, coming near
There falls another tear

Tyra G. McKellar
Frederick, MD

Our Mom

She's strong, gifted and intelligent.
She's fun, energetic, and always smiles.
She embraces life's challenges like a fighter in a ring.
She's the backbone of our family.

She cooked our meals and washed our clothes.
She cleaned our wounds and wiped our tears.
She survived our teenage years.
She cried at our weddings with happy tears.
She became a grandmother in the later years.

The time has come for her to rest,
as she has done her very best.

Although she tried to hide her pain,
Each breath she took we saw her strain.

Decision was made to say goodbye.
We watched her sleep and kissed her soft cheeks.
We held her hands and rubbed her cold feet.

Her lungs were broke and unable to mend.
We stayed with her until the end.

She looked so peaceful, tranquil and calm.
She's our angel, she's our mom.

Linda Fahey Doiron
Billerica, MA

My Door

I am waiting, that door is open
my messages are there, thru the image in you
I create you…. I know what you can give me
I am waiting, the door is open,
Where and how you enter thru that door is your choice,
your faith and hope will lead you.

The door is open, I am waiting
My blessing is there thru image in you.
Believing in you is receiving the faith
Listening my word thru image in you
Is…you coming home, were you born.

The door is open, I see you
You stop and look the other way
The image in you is me,
Wash yourself with my tears that I gave you,
Your thirst is my blessing.

There is nothing that you do, be paste by me
I am everywhere where you are.
The door is open, you are me
I am you, look to the blue sky, touch the water
Grab the dirt…the door of the garden is full of fruit.

Kaltrina N. Ventemiglia
Weatheford, TX

"Life is currency that should be spent on something that will outlast it." I learned this from my good friend, western artist, Chuck Dehaan. We create art, stories, news, and much more for one reason: to send a message to others. I have been living in America for the last twenty-five years. I lived through different windows of life. I've learned life is a gift from God. With hope and faith, He will be your shepherd. The reason I love to write is to bring light into people's lives. Word is a power . . . sometimes it can change the world . . . if it is the right word.

Buds

Where are we from? How do we know?
Isn't there something that could have made us?
Something could be watching us.
Why can't we see them or him or her?
Is there a reason for life or are we just here by mistake?
If we are a mistake, then how do we know the rest isn't as well?
What is supposed to be here?
Are we a mess-up and a throw-away?
Did we really need to be here and not somewhere else?
Do we have a purpose at all?
Is this a never-ending cycle or will it come to an end?
How will we ever know?
Could we just be a theory, actually a thought, not really living?
Why do we have emotions?
Do other living things have emotions too?
Will we ever know why we have to reproduce?
What happens if we choose not to? What happens if we do?
What's right? What's wrong? Who can really even say?
What will determine what is right and wrong?
How could you even begin to answer?
There couldn't be, could there?
Will the questions slow to a trickle instead of a pour?
Does life exist in a greater world?
Why do they think there isn't anything else?
Everything is something and even then, nothing is something too,
but how can we know what something actually is?

Samantha J. Triantafelo
North Mankato, MN

123

The Devil, My Dear!

Her beauty has moved more than mountains and seas
She's fooled me then ruled me in thousands of dreams
She's truly a newly made mistress each time
Inviting, exciting; still higher we climb
It's always the same, though, I can't see the end
Where the peak borders bleak, love and lust tend to blend
Still, I toe to the edge with the faith of a knight
For a foe, I have pledged I would faithfully fight
Every dark and demented enchantment we find
"Till we've ended in heaven, in the end, she'll be mine!"
All this I speak to myself on the brink
Of a pit, the abyss, where the doomed ever sink
And there I remember myself standing "here"
The rush of her touch leaves me clutching the fear
Moved by the unmoved, reduced to the mere
A fool to my true love, the Devil, my dear!

Colten R. Lyke
Bradenton, FL

Thinking of You

Thinking of you I find myself today
How lucky I am to have you as my friend
Thinking of you I smile at the things we've done
How wonderful it is to have someone to trust
Thinking of you my heart beats uncontrollably
How happy I am to know someone cares for me
Thinking of you I'm lost in my thoughts
How scared I am of falling in love

Thinking of you I still find myself today
It's great to know you're more than a friend
Thinking of you hoping you feel better
How can I tell you how much I really care
Thinking of you and wishing to be there
How wonderful it would be to fly like a bird
Thinking of you and saying little prayers
God willing, tomorrow we'll be together
Thinking of you and writing this little poem
I want you to know how much I really love you

Sonia Cepeda
Londonderry, NH

Remembering the Past

In my death
the darkness rises
through the mist
of endless lies

I swam endlessly through
the ocean of tears
to only see my deepest fears
My breath came ragged
like the cold wind through the trees
As I ran I could hear their howls
The souls of the dead
were after me

My breath caught in my throat
I could not breathe
My life was fading, fading
At last I came to the old home church
where I felt abandoned
and most hurt
I remembered the past
of endless pain
where shouts and screams
fell like rain

I ran some more
till I knew no more
I stumbled and limped
through the twisted forest
till at last I fell
My life was fading, fading
And in death
I am most strong
free from the toil and strife
of my long lonely life

Joshua L. Girven
El Dorado Springs, MO

126

Cut

Something triggers my mind
A word, a phrase, an action
Once it crosses my mind I have to
I race up into my room
Frantically I search for my tool
Something sharp
a needle, scissors, anything
It's in my hand
Pressure against my wrist
"You're a f***ing c***, you don't deserve to live"
More pressure
"How can you be so stupid?!"
Pain rushes through my arm
"I want to die"
I move down my arm
There's many lines now
I press the razor deep into my skin
Hoping for blood to seep around it
It's not working
I lightly carve into the pressured lines
I finally see blood
Tears fall
"No one cares about me"
More tears
I slowly lose grip and let the razor fall
Wishing it was over

Jennifer L. Olson
Pasco, WA

Mirrors of Your Life

Monsters of the valley, creatures of the sea
Come to me, come to me as far as you may be
The mirrors, you look into the mirrors, they will lie
Yet we all continue to look as our lives go by
One day you and future are going to collide
And you'll realize the only beauty there is
Is the beauty that lies inside

Clancy A. Gray
South Nyack, NY

My name is Clancy Gray, and I live in Nyack with my dad and stepmom. I also live in Tuxedo, NY with my mom. I am in 8th grade and am excited about entering high school next year. I have a sister, a stepsister, and a stepbrother. Their names are Morgan, Francessca, and Milo. My best friends are Stephanie and Christina (we call her Jojo). Many things inspired me to write this poem. One was when I was feeling bad about myself and the way I look. I base my poems on things that go through every thirteen-year-old girl's mind. Others, I just get an idea and go with it. I write poetry because it's what I like to do. It is also a great stress reliever; whatever is on my mind is turned into a poem, just like the one I have showed you. So this is my world and why I love to write poetry.

Go Home, Purity

The anvil of pain that lay upon my chest, stole my breath
surroundings blur and fade as I swallow my throat
the dullness in my heart throbs
I desperately suck for air
if only he could see the light . . .
experience the freedom, the peace

In the romantic essence of the darkness
He held every piece of my naked corpse
the morning breaks dawn
roughly, purposefully, flesh breaks free from the world of dreams
pure animalistic nature stands in for passion
Groggy flesh drives movement into the clouds of release

Monotone sounds of electronic politics fade into the distance
tenderness dissipates involuntarily
creating bursts of innate reality in which she abides
go home, purity. . .

Mary G. Heitman
Whitefish, MT

My Pale Moon

You burn like the sun
Not bright, but damaging
Not shiny, but blinding.
I am the moon
Not jeweled, but pale
Not intriguing, but a question.

I, the moon, yearn for your brightness
Your warmth, your light.
What holds me up are my stars, my dreams, my possibilities
But eventually I vanish
And then comes your turn
You, the leader, have power, but weakness.

The fact is you are my sun
I am your moon.
Blind all you want, take my sight,
Just let me keep my glow,
Take my sky, but don't take my glow.

Ilana Ortiz
Bronx, NY

Never Again

The light will never shine again
Never within my heart.
For terrible loss and horrible pain
Hath ripped it all apart.

Instead the darkness there shall reign
Encroaching on my heart,
Filling me with much disdain
For ripping us apart.

The love that used to keep me sane
That always warmed my heart,
Now is merely just the bane
That keeps me ripped apart.

You I shall never see again
The one who has my heart,
Your death has caused me terrible pain
And hath ripped my heart apart.

Nicolette T. Karls
Franksville, WI

Beacon

There is no escaping this light.
You may think yourself
Permanently rooted in darkness—
Having fallen down, down into
Into a cavernous, bottomless winter;
Possessed, then quieted like
Some wild animal who has
Finally given up the fight.

But then you are roused, wakened
To go out and scan the storm clouds
For any breakout streak of blue.

Or compelled to deep woods
Where you hunt feverishly
The tiny purple trillium
Whose face has lived in you
This cold season,
And now looks up with light
And splendor of a star.

One day the sun burns
Its glittering diamond fire
Across a nascent pond
Directly into your heart,
Surrendering to flame
There is no way to play dead.

Linda L. Fialkoff
Littleton, MA

A Love Like No Other

This love is no suicide
Our hearts are closed and tied
In this love, we might not get to touch
But to the other, when we talk, it means so much
This love we might not yet get to walk side by side
Yet we still are going strong and go along for the ride
This love makes us know where we belong
Our love makes strong
This love might not be able to kiss
But to have it, it is such a bliss
We might argue and shout
But I know we will always have each other, I have no doubt
This love we crossed roads
In my life I fell for some bad toads
In this love, I knew I loved you from the start
I trusted you with my heart
I can't wait for your skin to be next to mine
While our bodies will intertwine
In this love, I think of you every day
Sometimes I just love to enjoy your company so don't know what to say
I knew you loved me and my walls came down
On my bad days you are my clown
Everything is an understatement, just loss of words
But I love us, we are just dorks and nerds
On my boat of life, to my harbor, you are my light
With you on my mind, I will hold on tight
Our love is like a beautiful firework
We will never lose our spark
Darling, you shine brighter than any star
With our love, we are finding out who we are
Our love glows more than the moon
In our hearts lies a beautiful tune

Courtney E. Holland
Mayfield, PA

Flight of the Wolf

When you hear a whispering howl through the silent night's air
Then you feel a gentle brush of feathers not seen there
As the still wind passes by, you will always know I am forever near.

Death has not claimed me, it has freed me
My journey is not over, it has now begun
Until the serene moment we are reunited to run as one.

In blessed repose, I will wait, watch, guide, and guard
My vow to you made at birth, a mother's love is never undone
From cradle to grave and the life beyond, know I will always be there.

Nicki "Winged Wolf" Kulivan
West Lebanon, IN

When the Sky Cries

We hear her sorrow throughout the night
Her tears hit the cold pavement
The trees swing and sway in the harsh winds
the sky darkens like a beast in the night waiting to swallow the
young baby birds

She's angry, she wants to drown the world below her
She's sad because she knows she's bare and all alone
That's when the sky cries

Deseray Lara
Holland, MI

Hope Our Love Is True

Whenever you're around everything feels right,
and the words "I love you" are such a pleasant sound.
Yet I lie awake at night and I can't help but wonder if you really love me.
I want to believe our love is true even if it's not.
For you I smile, for you I breathe and it's worth the while if you
won't ever leave.
I want to believe our love is true even if it's not and if I wake before
I die,
my dying wish is you.

Misty M. Baughn
Corsicana, TX

I love writing poems about my life, myself, and everything around me. This poem
was inspired by my boyfriend, Aaron. He inspired me in so many ways. I have been
writing poetry since I was ten years old. Writing poetry is how I express myself.
My family is a big reason why I started writing. Also my boyfriends, whom I see as
my own. They have all inspired me.

Blind of It

If never the pain were to subside,
I would not mire in confusion of trying to hide
My hurt for it would not matter.
And then slowly, relentlessly, I died.

My memories are but only faded examples
Of something living, one of God's samples.
It's heart used to be red,
but now proclaimed dead, from painful tramples.

I think...I ponder...I feel I'm done,
Because nobody declared me a "loved one"
And especially, specifically that one girl
Who never knew, will never know,
How in my land, she was my resplendent Sun

Javier E. Martinez
La Habra, CA

Not Gonna Rain

I kiss the sun good morning
A smile on my face
No tears are escaping from my eyes
I'm right where I need to be
Happy as a girl can be
Nothing's going to get in my way
You're not gonna rain on my parade.

No Tears Goodwin
Archer City, TX

Sleep

Sleep,
Avoids me.
A restless leg.
And a restless mind.
I pray relief will come.
And bring the sweetness at day's end.
Must I endure the never-ending shifting?
When will I invoke the lord of dreams?
Deep gulf, I hear you calling as I reach
All the way down, till morning comes with its breach.

Robert De Cicco
Seattle, WA

I read somewhere about a form of a poem that has ten lines beginning with one word on the first line and proceeding to add one word to each additional line. So line two has two words and so on, ending with ten words on line ten. This intrigued me so I thought I'd give it a "go" and wrote "Sleep."

Your Essence

From the moment I saw,
Your Essence I thirst;
Just a slight swallow dear
Of your Essence I must.
Replenish and fill me,
With your sweetest of touch
Sweetest of smiles, I've never seen such.
Give me your Essence,
And I won't ask again;
All I ask is a cup
Of your Essence woman.
I saw you walking, and I saw your grin.
Just pour your sweet Essence
Upon me, friend.

Brent L. White
Eight Mile, AL

I am also known by the pseudonym Eye Q the Blac Poet, which is most noticeable in my debut book of short stories entitled *The Document*. *The Document* explores suspense in-depth and contains dynamic plot twists, elaborate concepts, multiple narrating forms, and unique characterizations that take on absurd perspectives. I attribute my desire to becoming a writer and poet to my passion for arts, which taught me to become more articulate, detail-oriented, and musical, which made me aware of rhyme and rhythm.

The Secret Life of a Dreamer

They say that dreams come true,
But only if you truly believe so.
Sometimes, if you just brush one aside,
It can come true, when you least expect it.

They say you have to work hard,
If you want your dreams to come true.
Sometimes you take one for granted.
Before you know it, it comes true

They say to go after your dreams,
That you can do whatever you set your mind to.
Sometimes, as much as you want the dream,
There may be too many obstacles.

Sometimes, the dream is in grasp,
So close, you can touch it.
But when reality gets in the way,
You have to stick with a real deal.

This is the life of a girl who's a dreamer.
One who believed, but went through the doubts.
The ups and downs of what it really is
To be a dreamer, and to have dreams,
But have the strength to hang on.

Carol F. Ladouceur
Deer Park, NY

Little Boy

Little boy so cute and tall
I will pick you up if you ever fall
If you are sad
I will make you glad
So have fun
And go in the sun
Jump around
As you drive around town
I am always here for you
So don't ever feel blue
Little boy so cute and tall
I will pick you up if you ever fall

Samantha M. Perrotta
Brookhaven, PA

One thing about myself is that I am an athlete. I like to play softball and basketball. My family is a big part of my life and they influence me to do a lot of good things. My inspiration for writing this poem was my nephew. He is precious to me and makes me feel happy.

Time to Choose

Light shimmers as the wind whips violently.
How can such beauty exist during such darkness?
Life flows in, out, in, out, as death peaks from the corner
Stay fast the end is coming.
What choice will you make?
The damnation of life or the salvation of death.

Theresa K. Pitts
Kountze, TX

the blood i crave

i am a slave
to the blood i crave
pouring it into a glass
dreaming of the past
craving every drop
i can't seem to stop
am i a slave
to the very blood
that i crave
or is this the end?
maybe a new beginning
my world is spinning
i am a slave
to the blood i crave

Jonathan Longcrier
Omaha, NE

Holding Back

Life…Life is for living. So why don't people live it?
We already know that we have one shot, one chance, one life.
So why do we hold ourselves back?
Fear…Why does fear take control?
Why do we want to feel safe?
Is being safe the same as being happy?
Or is it just a few seconds of pleasant feeling, with the aftertaste of
more fear?
Future…Is it destiny?
Is life written out, word for word, as it's meant to be, or is it what
you make it?
Can you stop it? Can you change it?
Fear, it's for the future.
The present. The past?
Disappear…What will tomorrow bring?
Can you get hit by a car?
Or hung from a string?
What will happen, when you're no more, people will forget you,
And Heaven is full?
Heaven…Is it really up there?
Or is it somewhere on Earth?
Somewhere you want to be?
Somewhere you rather be?
So why aren't you there yet?
Life…Why do we hold ourselves back?

Khushbu M. Patel
Norristown, PA

Feelings

I feel so lost
empty inside, why do we
Love just so they can die?
Why do we feel the butterflies
in the belly by just a single
touch, our faces turning red
when one embarrasses us, the
little smiles we shed when one
notices us, but most of all
we feel the Love.
We know it is there,
we love the way it feels,
and then one day
it's gone
a memory is all we have left.
"It is part of life" is something
I have heard yet it doesn't make
it easier nor stop the hurt.

Crystal D. Wade
Howard, KS

O My Daughter

"I hate you! I hate you!" she says
"You never understand me!" she says
"Why are you so mean to me?" she says

"What do you want from me?
You know I'm angry.
Can you just let me be?"

"No! I will not let you be.
You belong to me.
Even when you are angry."

"I will not give up on you," I said.
"Even when we argue," I said.
"So stick with me and together we will agree to get through," I said.

Tara N. Chin
Homestead, FL

Life of a Spartan

The pulse of my heart beats to the sound of the war horn
Adrenaline flows through my veins at mercurial speeds
The clangs of clashing swords and shields pierce my ears
The battle is lost, or though it seems

Thousands of them, 300 of us
The sight dismays our fighting hearts
To surrender is to lose, as is to press onward
Battle is virtue, death is an art

Our spirits burn brightly
Though dealt the wrong hand
Our strong will prevails
Our detriment, we withstand

The strength of a Spartan
No strength can compare
For we are the Spartans
Our surrender is rare

Max J. Gibson
Long Beach, NY

The Hardest Reality

Life is the hardest reality, the penitentiary is my life,
Trapped in this 8 x 9, I feel like dying, I can't see, there's no light.
Confined to endless time, a lone passenger on this long flight
How can I unwind my mind when I'm condemned to sleepless nights?
The cold and discomfort becomes second nature to me,
Getting old and forgotten, like a log washed up from sea,
The steel doors and wired fences assure I won't get free,
The concrete floor is all I know, can't feel carpet to my feet.
I'm the product of my past, what I have done has brought me here
How much longer can I last, that's a question I do fear,
Can't relax—any second death or danger could be near,
Can't take back what I have done, but even real men can shed tears.

Life is the hardest reality, the penitentiary is my life,
Kept in a dark cell while they wait for my demise.
Got me sitting here rotting as I watch the world go by
But they can't stop me from plotting all the dreams I have inside.
The walls are closing in, but my mind is expanding out,
God forgive me for all my sins, I know now what life's about.
Doesn't matter where I've been 'cause the place I'm facing now
allowed me to repent so I can plan for a better route.
Just like me, your life can be—just like a penitentiary.
What it means to be free goes beyond physicality,
If your mind is not at peace, freedom means no victory,
And in the end you will see that life is the hardest reality.

Ngoc Thai Kien
Tacoma, WA

The Life of Another

Boxed in, no expectation of escape.
This time, it is not the stillness
of life's passing, but of my own.

Might the honesty of life not be
what is captured in a photo,
or in the admired mixture of paint on canvas,
but in the moments mindfully discarded.

Where might be the experts
preparing future journeymen
for periods such that we'd prefer not to reach,
but stumble upon despite the direction of our quest.

Instead, may our fate be forever
interrupted by that of loss
accompanied by a false awareness
that a life of struggle cannot be good enough
for anyone's standards.

Kalolaine A. Palei
Salt Lake City, UT

Moonlight

There is a twist
At midnight, so scary
They'll give you a fright
they screech and scream
All through the night
They fly amongst us
Though we do not see
They are white and
Shine beneath their scales
They creep down from above
With more than 73 calls
They are called
Mongolian Screamers

Michelle A. Layne
Modesto, CA

Going Back

If I could go back and free the pain
There would be no remorse and would be no shame
For the times I ran, for the times I stumbled
For the ones I tripped, they would see me humbled
It's all a lie, it's me as a fake
It's about forgiveness, for my soul's sake
I have found the way
For this better day
My future is bright, I followed the light

Marsha B. Traughber
Springfield, TN

A Slip of the Lip

Here is a question that I ask of you:
What could there possibly be for me to do?
Oh I know now what could be done,
for my mind has finally spun, and now begins my world of fun.
I could race someone up a snowy mountain,
or just walk over to the water fountain.
My mind frolics side to side,
spreading its arms just as willing as the eagle that can glide.
This brain ushers secrets, it sputters nonsense,
it knows the light, and it knows the dark.
With no sign of stopping it pours from faucets,
continuing to condense into golden lockets.
I see images of creatures that bite and bark,
as well as a woman with no sight
who paints grand pictures of Tony Stark.
An usher of madness makes me feel unique,
for one must be slightly insane to fill the world's critique.
Here I am writing such an odd rhyme and alas, I feel....
I no longer have time. I must bid you farewell,
until next we meet, ha-ha,
but only God will tell of what we may have to feat.
Farewell, adieu, and good-night to you.

Jeffery R. Totty
Rogers, TX

Dressed in All Black

I didn't raise a murderer; America did. You see I had all the right intentions to raise my boy into a man. We have failed! It takes a village to raise a child, especially going up against the streets which have become far too wild. Influenced by what they see on TV the tangible things instead of the everlasting knowledge which can be endured by a schooling system who can't even seem to lure our children off the streets. A place that they've made their home in replace to decease what is really going on back home. A lack of parenting throughout the community, but hey, we can't all blame them; they're only teaching what their parents taught to them. A never-ending generation of violence that our children seem to be immune to. Our idols have no idea the influences they've ensured. Ensuring that we stay one step behind in a system designed to have us hate one another resulting in crime. A system made for us to fail. And we have accomplished what that very system had entailed. Failed! In our community using our intended inspirational centers as fighting grounds and the sales of drugs which leads to the narcotic usage behind the playgrounds our children use. We are at war in our community and you look at me like I'm the enemy. No! Blame the media! Corrupting our children's premature minds that they should settle and hustle and grind! No! Blame the government putting more funds toward the stereotypical planning sports! No! Blame our elders for giving up on us way too long ago looking the other way instead of saying, "Hey! Bring your butt this way." So today I am dressed in all black because, like my son, we are dressed in a color designed to hate one another which eventually leads to us eliminating each other one by one until we finally realize the real accomplishment! Wiping out a color so deep, that endured pain so we could reach our peaks! A plan set by the man as he sits back and watches us unknowingly follow his commands. This is no fib, I didn't raise a murderer; America did!

Dominique Ella Latonya Jones
Chicago, IL

Falling

Falling through ice
feeling shivery cold
Fingers skim the surface,
toes touch the grained sand...
struggling to breathe and shimmy
on to the ice to find warmth

Crackling fire is all that plays in my head,
need for warmth stings my naked body.
Tingling toes, fumbling finger,
I pull myself out with ounces of strength.

Lying bare against the thin ice
Unable to; to feel the cold
I breathe frosted air.

Slowly cold consumes me,
covers me like a blanket.
I'm seeing night without a moon;
Total darkness.

Brittany J. Worcester
Winterport, ME

On Earth

On this earth we all must be.
So why not love and harmony?
Instead of all the war and hate
We all deserve a better fate.
Stamp out hunger, make air clean
Water that's blue, grass that's green.
A better day for you and me
Is all that we want to see.
But all the politics, greed and waste
Leave you with a bitter taste.
For this is our world and land
And must be shared by every child, woman and man.
It is not perfect and never will be
And people are different from sea to sea.
But it is up to us to try to preserve this land
That God left in our hands.

Oliver L. Cantrell
Atlanta, GA

Stolen Innocence

Me and my little sister loved to have fun,
We loved to run around and play in the sun.
We did everything little girls liked to do,
For what was in store we had no clue.
Mommy had a new boyfriend who was really nice,
He said little girls were made out of sugar and spice.
Mommy would dress us up and put make up on us,
And send us in there like beauty queens and we weren't allowed to fuss.
He said he wanted to play a game,
And when we were done he said we would feel like fame.
We were really good and tried not to cry,
When it was done I wanted to die.
I didn't quite understand I was only four,
All I could do was fall to the floor.
Mommy I thought you loved me,
Now I just wish you could see.
I had to grow up quick with no defense
Because of my stolen innocence.

Tabitha N. Couchman
Peru, IN

My inspiration for my poem "Stolen Innocence" came from my father. He was diagnosed with stage four cancer on September 10, 2010, and passed away December 6, 2010. Before he left this earth I wanted him to know the love and appreciation I have for him for saving us from this horrible nightmare. I would like to dedicate this poem to my loving father, Phil. I love you, Daddy!

Scarecrow Serenade

One nation, under surveillance.
With liberty for some,
And about as much justice as the dead presidents will allow.
We hold this truth to be self-evident.
That all men are not created equal.
Your rights and freedoms are dicatated by a lie.
Apart from God's help,
The pursuit of happiness will result in death and taxes.
Scarecrow, you want a revolution?
What is this copy of a solution?
Might look good on paper,
Even sound great to the raper.
You, in the amber, from mountain to plain.
Silent sentinel, standing still in the snow and rain.
Yeah, I stutter like a prisoner,
Heck no, nothing like a minister.
This land is still called America.
Pushing and shoving, pulling and loving.
From the crash of industry, to the machine called computer.
Scarecrow, let me set the table, and be able to have food.
Apart from this serenade.
Away from you Scarecrow.
Having it made, far and away from a passing grade.

Thomas J. Dunahay
Northglenn, CO

A Dusty Book on the Shelf

I feel like a closed book,
Hiding on a library shelf,
The one no one ever checks out,
Because the title is boring,
Just a simple autobiography,
Lacking in plot and in detail,
And the cover just the same.
But I've got news for you,
I may be a book on a shelf,
But I'm full of illustrated pages,
With lengthy explanations,
And a list of oxymorons.
I go against the normal view,
I defy all stereotypes,
Yet I'm not a best seller.
I'm glanced over in disinterest,
My spine remaining always intact.
Still I'm yearning for someone
To take a look,
Read a paragraph,
Understand me better,
Because I'm not as boring as I seem.
I'm complex and lengthy,
But I provide a good read.

Mercedez G. Bradley
Omaha, NE

Moon

The silver glow of the moon was etched into the lake
Shivering slightly as waves rippled past
The mystery of it all still presided
As it lit up the surrounding area
A leaf fell onto its surface
Engulfing parts of the image into a shadowy depth
It started to paint a whole new scene
Creating mountains and rivers
It did not stop until the sun came out
Poking its head up above the horizon
And chasing the moon from out of the sky
The next night, it would come back again
Allowing new landscapes to be formed
New pictures to be drawn
New mysteries to be unraveled

Lisa Douglas
Lake Oswego, OR

Dandelion

Not considered a beauty,
plain and simple,
we're told it's a weed.
This flower of innocence.

This flower of youth
not a rose
nor daisy or buttercup.
This flower of innocence.

Golden in the sun,
made wreathes by the flaxen hair
for faux-kindergarten weddings
and monkey-bar May-days.
This flower of innocence.

As you grow older
that flower changes,
matures,
ready to sow life into the world.
This flower of innocence.

A transfer of hands,
a changing of seasons,
blown away—
creating others.
This flower of innocence.

Jessica Martin
Millers, MD

I Will Not Bow

Vibrance beats in every color of this dream
Lost images in high contrast blend with a new light
Shedding shadow on the life of the dying
Memories that thrive in the valleys of the mind
Flowing down neural mountains behind depthless eyes
Skin shudders in remembrance of the missing
Pleasure targets the weak to flourish
Watch the strong crumble under the breath of the vanished
No thing withstands the torrents of reminiscence
Features so bright in the light of the fictitious
Tremble in the face of desires that breathe in the lands of the lost
So grasp at that which eludes all touch
Wake in the light of a crushing weight
Waves from the oceans of the yearning crash and subside
Beating raw the wounds exposed by heedless dreams
An enemy in the solace and reprieve of sleep
As the closing of fevered eyes shocks to sight the visions
Pounding upon the grieving heart
Do not offer me this hope while my mind is vulnerable
A beautiful dream flitting tantalizing in front of my grasping fingers
To slip away in the morning sun
Night terrors no longer residing in dark recesses of the night
Choosing to haunt in the waking hours of a breaking soul
You torment the living by loving the dreamer
Preference to wade against the current of the grieving
Versus living forever in the forests of the past
I will rise above your dreaming hope
Hopeless dreams that aid the haunting
To torment the haunted in their waking state
I will rise above your memory
Gracing my dreams with the hope of my desires
Only to take away that which was so desperately accepted
Waking to a world where dreams are but shadows
I will not break under the storm of your haunting words
I will not cringe before the thunder of your provocative hope
I will not bow under the hail of your bruising ghost
I will not close my eyes against the glare of your burning presence
I will not fall before your memory.

Carly J. Anderson
Warrenton, VA

My Dear Mother

All you mothers out there
whether you are far or near
I just want to say
Happy Mother's Day

My dear mother went to her heavenly home
That is where she now roams
It seems like yesterday
But her memories are here with me to stay

So all you mothers out there
whether you are far or near
I hope you are loving your children, one and all
So that they will have good memories to recall.

Sonia R. Colbert
Omaha, NE

My Brothers

Today is the day that my brother was born
But I am so sad because my mother was so torn.
He lived eleven days,
which made the last day such a daze
By then came my brother, Eric, Kyle's twin, which I was so amazed.

We were all so sad but we knew it was for the best
Which brought each and every day to be such a test.
He has gone away to a better place,
Which we now know he is really safe.

He will always be in our heart
and we love him very dear.
But it is time to say goodbye,
And we will always know he is near.

Goodbye Kyle, we love you.
            Eric, I am so glad you're here.

Tylor M. Erdman
Millersburg, PA

My Prayer for Marcy

From deep within my heart I pray to you,
oh God above,
and ask one special thing of you,
please watch the one I love.
I cannot hold her, give her love,
or even hear her fears.
And only you, oh God above,
can wipe away her tears.
Please help her in her trials of life,
and always let her know,
she has a place within my heart
with a never-ending glow.
She's in my heart, my mind and soul,
she's my eternity.
As time goes on, and life gets hard,
please let her remember me.
When I get back, I'll hold her near
and keep her by my side.
But as for now, dear God above,
in you I must confide.

I only ask one thing of you,
please watch the one I love.
From deep within my heart I pray,
to you oh God above.

Anthony E. Richardson
Spring Valley, CA

The Creole Princess

Creole Princess with copper skin.
Oh! you look so fine.
You are shaped like an hour glass.
Your lips so plump with lust.
Your art is full of grace, dreaming of liberty.
Creole Princess with lustrous hair
Oh! you smell so good.
Your face sparkles as the morning light.
Your eyes bright as a sunny day.
You fought the freedom war.
The bell of victory rang,
and the flag of Independence was raised.
Creole Princess with perky breasts Oh!
Your smile is beautiful.
Your touch so soft and gentle.
You stand tall.
Proud as a revered queen.
Unaware what lies ahead, screaming Liberty!
Equality! And Fraternity!
Oh, negro woman you speak too loud.

Margareth Debrosse
Valleystream, NY

I reside in Valleystream, NY. I have three beautiful children—Reginald, Raquel, and
Antoine Jr.— and a wonderful husband, Antoine Jean-Joseph. I'm a compassionate,
caring, and sensible person with a burning love for humanity. I've been working
as a nurse for fourteen years. What inspired me to write the poem "The Creole
Princess" is my country Haiti. I was watching a documentary about Haiti's history
on January 12th, the anniversary of that catastrophic earthquake that tore parts of
the country apart, and after viewing the documentary, I couldn't stop asking what
happened to Haiti, a country that once was called "La Perle Des Antilles" (The Pearl
of the Antilles). It is deplorable to see what has become of the country today. To
me, Haiti is "The Creole Princess."

Orange

A round orange
Grew in size—
Was bound and deranged.
One day decided
To wear a gown, and
Quickly dropped on bench
Right underneath the orange tree
The best get closer to the ground…
Last night I've seen a clown:
The round orange wore a gown,
On country range, uptown.

Larysa Kochel
Hurst, TX

Alone

Every day I go through Hell,
When everyone is good and well.
I walk through pain and despair,
but no one cares.
As I go through life, a loner,
all everyone sees is an organ donor,
but I walk this road
with agony in more loads.
So I end with this,
my loneliness is my bliss.

Zachery P. Brown
Box Elder, MT

My Prayer for Her

She gives me meaning, a reason to care
Breath to my body, she is my air.
Lowly and humble, down on my knees
Asking the Lord to please hear my pleas.

I ask Him for guidance and the right words to say
Praying for her, as I do every day.
Please watch over her, with your goodness and grace
Please give her strength, with things she must face.

Open her heart, with a place there for me
How much I care for her, let her eyes see.
Let her feel the love, I have in my heart
Always for her, even as we're apart.

Please give her wisdom, to know right from wrong
And the comfort I offer is where she belongs.
Fill her with happiness and joy in her life
No grief or sadness, no pain or no strife.

Hear me O' Father, with the words that I pray
Bless her forever and protect her each day.
My love's never-ending, she's all things to me
She's in my heart and always will be.

Bill Henderson
Johnson City, TN

Precipitation

He touches everything uncovered,
like dew or frost at dawn.
He dictates our daily plans.
He's the King and we're the Pawn.
He's the brother of Ms. Sunshine,
and the fraternal twin of Snow.
With the help of her heated rays,
he causes seedlings to grow.
The blister of Wind
will make him chilly and more wet,
but he holds our world together
like a natural net.
From season to season
in the heat and the cold,
he's Mother N.'s favorite son,
the chief of the fold.
This place of highest honor
is not free it costs a ton.
She calls on him most often
when the job must be done...
to relieve the earth from Drought
or start the cycle of new life,
every year when he mates
with Spring, his longtime wife.

Monet M. Wheatley-Phillip
Jacksonville, FL

I am currently pursuing a Master of Arts degree in English. I am happily married and we have one daughter. I am a member of the Florida Writer's Association. I am the former editor-in-chief and current poetry contributor to the *Rising Sun Monthly* newsletter for the Dayspring Baptist Church in Jacksonville, Florida. I plan to continue writing and I am currently working on a novel. My writing style is simple. I enjoy writing about basic themes: nature, family, and everyday experiences. I have penned a self-help book *Pregnancy and Child Birth*.

Crash

As the cars come to a crashing halt
The driver wonders, who's at fault
Did I run a stop sign that I did not see
Was he texting someone and just didn't see me

What should I do, is anyone hurt
Questions race my mind, till I see a woman lying in the dirt
I can't move, my legs are pinned
As I look around and notice blood pouring from my best friend

The other car is upside down in the ditch
I wish I could change the last 2 minutes with a flip of a switch
I would take my time, maybe stop for a bite
Instead my buddy may be dead; it's a hell of a sight

I hear the sounds from far away
It's an ambulance or cop to save the day
They need to hurry I start seeing smoke
Oh god, my cars on fire, I'm starting to choke

Please God save me, I'm too young to die
As all these fears in my mind ask why
Why is it me, what have I done
I was on my way to a party to have a little fun

The ambulance got there just a little too late
The car was engulfed with flames, and on this date
Three people died and that's all we know
It's a warning for all to start driving slow

Timothy S. Rawlins
Erin, TN

166

Cowardly Silence

An over-analyzation, from blood to bone,
the choice was earth, or bleed alone.
Once so close, yet close so far,
words and such to stab me with stars.
Bleed the gold or bleed alone,
sunk so far in blood unknown.
The choice was up, she ripped her tongue,
to never come home, she ripped undone.
To lie from front, to lie to back,
never bleed home to keep intact.
Ripped unbleed to tongue unknown?
Feelings left, bled, to never have shown.
But the way she felt inside,
to never have known, leave me uncried.
To starch the bones and creed the fight,
cross the fort and lead by night.
A mind evolved, unshunned, unfold,
Un-thousand tales to scream untold.
To die in arms, a crowded mind,
too lazy to be genius to cry, unbind.
A gift dead precious, a lusty steed,
to bleed un-cried, or cry un-bleed?
A neck bone so gorgeous, such beautiful structure,
so strong, yet unable to ever have f***ed her.
To ruin, so closed, so open, so closed,
Deserving? Let never, she never yet chose.

Caitlin L. Merkel
Finksburg, MD

167

Hidden Truth!

A secret hidden behind torment and pain
was told to me today,
Hidden behind tears and many beatings.

I could see the tears ready to fall out,
out of his beautiful blue eyes,
Though they were held in to look tough,
not to look like a sissy,
I listened to my fiancé today,
listened to him tell me of his childhood,
I learned he had a hidden secret,
a secret no one else had a clue about,
It went so deep he paused after every word,
paused to forget the many beatings he faced......

Cassandra R. Jennings
Bourbon, MO

This Mind

This mind, my mind.
It thinks...but what?
These thoughts I have, what are they?
   They're passionate, yet sad, bold, and simple.
   They're strong, yet cold, mad, and complex.
They make no sense.
   They are a loop. They run through my head, and yell.
Yell so loud, and yet I can't seem to really hear them.
Why do I think the way I do? I look at my life and it's sad.
I can't imagine true happiness, but why?
I want my thoughts to be different. I want my life...this loop, to be
   different.
   How do you break a thought? How do you change the way you
   think?
How do I control my mind...switch the wiring in my head, and
   change this loop?

Lisa-Marie Burnside
Burbank, CA

My Sisters Three

She is strong and beautiful;
She deserves the very best.
She is smart and special;
Better than the rest.
She's the one I'd talk to
If I didn't keep it locked inside.
She's the one I'd tell
If I could swallow my pride.
She's the one who sees me
And knows me way down deep.
She's the one who loves me,
And from her, secrets I can't keep.
She's the one who sticks up for me,
Who always has my back.
She's the one I'd die for
Without having to think a sec.
She is my sister;
My sisters they are three,
Faith Ann, Sarah Elisabeth, and Victoria Leigh.
And I just wanted to tell you,
To tell you all three,
That I'd give my life for you
And the air that I breathe.
Forever and always,
I will love you 'till then.
My love is permanent
Like the ink of a pen.
Forever you can count on me;
Always you will see
That I love you the best;
My Sister's Three.

Charity McKinney
Abbeville, GA

I am eighteen years old and I am from south Georgia. Until two years ago, I had never written a poem. One day I sat down and wrote my feelings on paper and when I was finished it was a poem. This poem was inspired by my three sisters. I wanted to tell them how much I loved them and no matter where life took me they would still mean the world to me. I hope you all enjoy this and can somehow relate to it. God bless.

Pain

Look at what you did to me
my heart is still bleeding
from the pain you caused
now I can't sleep at all

My eyes filled with tears
this pain is going to hurt for years
why did you do this to me
I hate what happened can't you see

Look at me again
I see you have that big grin
Grin on your face
your lying is such a waste

Waste of time
when you committed the horrible crime
the crime of painful hurt
now that I have seen that you're a crazy jerk

See you gone
away from your home
away from me
until then I will just let you be

Shampyne S. Johnson
Baytown, TX

Manifestations of a Warped Reality

You know who you are,
the person who so strives to demoralize
and further criticizes anything anyone ever does,
serving their demise on silver platter with a side of denies.
Not meeting expectations, refusing to look at calculations,
manifestations that further control your selfish limitations,
only to further push away relations and all of the considerations
that you've had for these precious recommendations.
But here I stand taking all the hits, lookin' at me like I'm a hypocrite.
You need to stand back and look at the benefits
that further commit themselves to you,
because with every eclipse light is only shown brighter,
and with every door closed there's a door that opens wider.
Take two steps back and look at the possibilities
because, guess what? No one can fly like frisbees,
No one holds your heart's keys, do you even have a heart?
Doubt it with all the lies you've spread, all your trustees
Because you are a wilting flower
forcing me to be cutting ever deeper into my soul,
squirting out knowledge and passion as the blood runs.
Are you finally happy knowing that my guilt is never resting?
You've made your own bed, now you must sleep in it
with sheets that are cheap and hard to upkeep.
Keep that silence of yours and count your sheep,
for it is I who weeps in the silent chaos just waiting to out leap.
But a wilting flower can be replenished
with every passing memory of us cherished
has seemed to have vanished in your black pit.
Flourished and nourished is what I am.
Can't you follow along?
Because when a flower blooms more people start to assume
all the many tombs they have dug for others to fall in,
but your message speaks nothing but volumes
with all the fumes that only cloud your warped view of the world.
All you need is to heed my words and repent
and go get a heart that's not for rent.
I'll stand by you 100 percent through the new world that you invent
because all the days spent on your cruelty has come and went.
So stand up and run like hell.
Now is not the time to turn away and rebel.
Take my hand and don't look back to dwell
on all the past you're leaving behind
because in your life, you are the inkwell, and life is your canvas
Because, you know that bed you made?
Someone else is already sleeping in it.

Marisa V. Herrera-Keehn
Santa Rosa, CA

I Am Home

Warmth consumes me.
The feel of a cool breeze ignites my senses as it crawls over me.
I can smell the sea salt in the air.
My body gravitates towards that smell,
like an addiction.
Fiery, electrifying sand squishes between my toes,
the gentle wind plays with my hair,
and the sun gazes upon me as I walk toward this phenomenon.
My eyes are entranced by the beauty ahead of me, and then I feel it.
The rush of cool water wraps around my ankles,
pulling me further into my fixation.
A steady current guides me while my feet explore the mysteries
below.
Waves surround my figure, and I dance to their beat.
My soul is gladly captured in the astonishment of the ocean.
I am home.

Alaina L. Hartman
Cincinnati, OH

Fragile Heart

Fragile is the status of my heart
The thought of loving, but not possibly being loved
Tears My Soul Apart
The thought of being none

Your hugs say one thing
But Your Mind Might say the other
How to know? Do you know how I feel?
Or is it just a way to break me apart?

Your presence brings me joy
Your "I Miss Yous" do too
But when I reply: "I miss you too"
I mean it, do you?

When the Angels aren't watching
I cry and pray for you
To Feel the way I do
But if the opposite is presenting
I swear I'll "Die" for you

Because of you, it's coming apart
My emotions, my strengths, and weaknesses too
If your response is "No," I don't want you at my "Funeral"
To see me crash because of you, because of my fragile heart.

Jennifer Garcia
Dublin, TX

Guide Me

While drinking tea
or taking a breath
allowing me
to let it be.
Guide me
so I may see
the beauty
that is there for me.
Allowing me
to let it go.
Breathing, releasing
and enjoying the flow,
while I grow.
And I may know
my inner peace
so I will continue to glow.

Heidi M. Macalpine
Manorville, NY

Heidi resides on Long Island, New York with her husband Ray and their three children. She is an occupational therapist and teacher who works with clients on becoming independent. She has been teaching Yoga to children and adults for over six years. She spends her free time enjoying various water activities, such as scuba diving, boating, and swimming. Her inspiration for writing poetry started with her passion for teaching and providing therapy to children. Her first poem "Empower Us" was published in *Anthology Perspectives*, which is poetry written on perspectives of autism and learning disabilities.

Ordinary Anomalous

I sit in a dark abyss caged by my own volatile mind.
My tears dripping down like rust cascading from an old wagon
forgotten in the limitless rain.
Society driving my chasm of anguish, I wipe the corrosion away
     from my untainted skin.
I often feel uncommon and unique in a colorless world,
but no one sees this solitary truth I feel within the depths of my heart.
It is as if I am a lotus flower surging up through the muck and dirty
     pond water.
People's iron eyes focus in only one direction.
They behold the unclean pond when they gaze.
There is no malice there. There is no hatred, there is only mere
     indifference.
A pond is seemingly ordinary. In this way, the world depicts their
     view of me.
But when I play this out in my mind, my frustrations ease and I smile
     to myself.
For, I am not the pond itself but rather the Lotus within it.
Only someone of true depth and insight will notice the beauty within.
I rise out of the lines of insanity and trail the wagon through the rain.

Aimee E. Cote
Belchertown, MA

Recycling Saves the Earth (But It Kills Me)

I don't know what it feels like anymore,
When things are right.
I can't even tell you if my heart works correctly,
But then, I hardly doubt it;
You dislodged it,
Crumpled it,
Tore at it;
My paper heart.
You lectured and ridiculed and reduced everything I thought I knew
    into a
1x1x1 ft. cube you could handle, and change, and toss back at me.
Solid, tangible, but so unreal.
Recycled romance.
You're so predictable you know,
But you think you're the most wild thing out there.
Chalk tears spill down my face,
Powdery regret dusting everything with its numbing silk.
You watch as the blackboard turns white.
Sometimes wanting happiness isn't enough,
Sometimes loving you just doesn't make the
Cut.

Maggie I. Coons-Abbott
Willits, CA

Sick of Poverty

I watch as the shadows of the trees disappear
My surroundings come alive
Ignorance controls the minds of those captured by poverty
No clear path and no real guidance
Only the convincing picture of the finer life
Bring hope into their eyes
Life with nothing but penny filled cups and white lines
The symptoms of it all
Are misconstrued as a sickness
And the meaning is often interchanged with a cause
Judgment is pressured upon and still the bigger picture is overlooked
The effect of oppression
Resulting in crimes committed
The untreated symptoms has escalated
Escalated into irreversible conditions of ignorance
But the means of the actions are enabled by the sickness
And still there're no reforms coming
To correct the defects of the misdiagnosed souls

Nydia S. Franklin
New York, NY

Living Life in Love

They go to bed in the dead of night waiting for the sun's intense light
Starving as they draw weary time passes on for them long and dreary
Every morn they walk shoeless in the dust and dirt watching the
world for themselves lost and hurt
They look around wondering what they'll do; no friends, no family,
just one life they pursue
Every time new refugees come to the camp they expect the same
very thing: disappointment
While many are safe along with others amongst their toil, free from
the wars plaguing the African soil
Many are left weeping in bittersweet tears knowing they had been
rescued when for others death had persevered
Nightmares, lost hopes, and far-gone dreams torment their minds--
young and old never to be spoken, never to be told
Seclusion and survival is the key for some it seems, it's too late for
breakthroughs and how it blasphemes
Life is no longer a reason to celebrate but to inquire of God for them
death's angel would take
Wake up to a day that never gives them reward back for until the
day's ending will they lounge on that hard bedrock of a homemade shack
They still smile thanking the Lord for His mercy but their eyes
expose how they feel life has cursed thee
So why do we nitpick about the lesser in existence growing greedy
and hypnotized by the market's increasing hindrance
As you witness and consider the lives of the deprived, desperate,
and suffering remember what you can do as relief to bring about the
recovering
Live a life of giving back let it be worth living for the God of
Heaven wants these precious ones breathing
Let your heart flourish in deep love and pour in to send that very
love to a needful orphan

Kristen Jefferson
Kyle, TX

An Ending

Each tear burns
I cannot cry
My stomach churns
I wonder why.

My head aches
I cannot see
My hearing breaks
How could this be?

Each whip stings
My blackened heart
More strength this moment brings
For with this thought I cannot part.

And then I feel better
No longer in pain,
God sent me a letter
That surged through my veins!

A feeling of love
Overflowing with healing
In the black, a white dove
Now I am so willing.

I yearn to fly with you
My heart needs tending.
Oh, can this be true
Is this our happy ending?

Teleysha B. Womack
Saint Johns, AZ

Ballad for Many You Still the Dream

Whew! At nights duke slumbers in cotton sheets.
The mortal reads lyrics, favors pleasures of existence.
Disquiets, shifts, has flashbacks of the beloved.
He disguises his bed as his sanctum.

Phone rings, doff, duke rejoinders the phone with melancholy.
Is this any that he'd faisted on to audit who is on the other dash?
That spoker is not the beloved.
Ye, the duke purposes to be confined with the y'clepter tomorrow.

In the after the two confronted sitten in a company.
The duke shakes hands with the fellow as is.
They pitched in the conversion and chat chat.
The two recited, "goodbye!" to each other vehemently.

Duke in woe, shoulders he sobs, a week has whiled away.
He hasn't heard from his swain, how come?
He is shaking; he can't go on like this undivulgedly.
He's undithered, in despair spot to do something!

Duke's existence beckons her in the glory zone.
He calms himself, he dejutioned, hurt and neglected.
His vigoring memoirs of her maketh earl worth much.
He is for so many reasons ardent to her enrichen soul.

Duke digs English betoken earls, doesn't he?
He is subduedly but yet: in meek love with her.
He thinkens he is worthy of her, she thinkens she is worthy of him, too.
However, they've reencountered; despairing duke says rend me no more!

Jacqueline Akopyan
Van Nuys, CA

181

Fingerprints

Surrounded by family
In a room full of flowers
Shedding tears and sharing stories
Of the one we just lost

Lining up for hugs and small talk
I took my final inhale
As I prepared for unfamiliar faces
To express their deepest sympathy

The people starting to flow in
Stopping to say their last good-bye
I noticed a certain imprint
That seemed to appear as they walked by

Many memories were shared
Some made me laugh, others just a grin
But all shared the same theme
She has helped many hands

As I said my final farewell
My tears began to flow
I kissed her hand one last time
And her fingers began to glow

Her fingerprints were left
On every hand she helped
Every heart she mended
And everything she touched.

Holly L. Brandewie
Minster, OH

The Surprise

My eyes are open
Yet I cannot see
Nor I blind
For there is light beyond me

Traveling so far
Yet so far away
The light I see
But no closer to me

The never-ending journey
An everlasting story
Until I close my eyes
My life, the surprise

Brandon K. Rogers
Rocky Mount, NC

Death Is Life

Death is Life. Life in another World.
The end of a New Beginning, away from Earth sinning.
Now, you up above, smiling and grinning...
You are with *God*!
That is a *Real* beginning. . .
For those that don't understand, you're disappearing.
They will understand in due time, because This World *End*
Is Nearing. . .
You just got a Headstart. . .
God is smart. . .
You have always had a Heavenly Heart!

Yolanda S. Hubbard
Old Bridge, NJ

The inspiration and motivation for this poem was my friend of twenty-three years.
I wrote it to her for the passing of her mother; Moma Scott had a beautiful heart!
It's poetry comforting for the soul; and that was my goal, to comfort my friend and
her family's souls! When someone dies/passes away, for their loved ones, what do
you do? What do you say? So, I wrote this poem for Rashida Scott-Cruz, for my
condolences, in my own way. I didn't know what else to do or to say.

Jesus

There is a King named Jesus
He really is for all of us
On a heavenly throne He lives
His message of salvation is to forgive

Jesus wants us to understand Him and love
For His is the perfect sacrifice from above
What profit has a man to have war and strife
When Jesus came to the earth to give eternal life?

Jesus has all of the honor, glory and fame
Because for sins He suffered over and over again
To say He does not have compassion and truth
Is to not understand that for remissions of sins He is the root

Jesus sits at the right hand of God with a crown
When we cry in pain, He picks us up from the ground
We are but part of the earth made by God's grace
Won't it be wonderful to finally see Jesus' face?

Eternity is such an endlessly long time
The length expands beyond the human mind
The gentle, kind, loving nature of Jesus helps us do the math
Jesus' father, God, gave us the Bible to lead the steps of our path

Our life is a journey in which Jesus carefully will watch
When we sincerely turn to Him, his Father will no more remember
our faults
Keep traveling with faith and hope in your heart
Jesus will never leave your side or depart

Sandra K. Riley
Newport, AR

The inspiration for this poem is the fact that Jesus is our Savior. He is the only
religious figure who actually died for humanity's sins. Jesus has helped me in my
life through tremendous difficulties. He has been a precious and dear friend in times
of need. Jesus' example on the earth can guide us on how to conduct our lives on
a day to day basis. Jesus is the King of Kings and Lord of Lords. Jesus is King
yesterday, today, and tomorrow. Jesus is eternally pure.

The Sound of Awe

As the morning star glows
Brighter with each passing instant
The shadows of the ever-rolling hills
Collapse

Dew dangles from the very tips of
Razor-bladed green grass
My breath is chilled
By the innocence of night's remainder

I crossed that old, tattered bridge
And in looking down, I witness
The elegant transformation of rippling transient stone
Deep coal colored chrome
Majestically paves itself down that
Rocky, rumbled, riverbed

Two logged trees are struggling,
Stuck on the pedestal of a trestle
Fighting the current, they ruffle the water
Mixing the gold and pink
Flakes of the early morning
Dawned sunlight with the
Coal colored chrome

I listen to the heavy rippling
Liquid metal as it
Reverberates off nature

And echoing in response
The sound of awe

Bryanna D. Mathias
Big Timber, MT

What If?

I like you and want you to know,
but I'm afraid to let these feelings show,
afraid to tell you how I feel,
afraid of everything that I feel.

I don't understand this,
why'd it have to be you?
I have some questions
that won't take long at all.
I doubt I'll ever know the answers
that I've been seeking for so long.

What if this isn't real,
these feelings I have for you?
What if when I get to the top I fall and crash and burn?

I don't want to fall like that,
fall and get real hurt.

I want to fall for you,
hoping you feel the same way, too.

I know this may sound corny,
I don't mean for it to,
but all I'm trying to say
is that I hope you feel the same way, too.

Austin M. Hayes
Green, OH

Life

Life is running out in the rain, no matter the consequences.
Finding happiness in even the worst circumstances.
Riding the highest roller coaster despite being scared,
Because your best friend wants to be paired.
Running barefoot in the snow
Because someone told you to go.

Life is crying when you feel like it.
If you don't want to run, just bike it.
Life is experiencing the pain,
Just to gain and maintain.
Life is saving your best friend from poor mistakes,
Because he or she is what keeps your world from a quake.
Life is when you erase disastrous thoughts
To replace them with adventurous ones that aren't distraught.

Life is climbing to the peak of that metaphorical mountain,
Just to prove that there is a fountain,
A fountain of solace and serenity,
One filled with all the amenities.

Life is chasing the girl of your dreams,
Because in the end you know you'll be connected like a seam.
Life's doing what's right,
Even if it takes all night.

Life is taking every chance,
Even if it's just the first glance.
If the road's too long, jog.
In the end, someone will be there to clear the fog.

Alex C. Miller
Norwalk, IA

Moon

The sky was lit by the moon's ominous trance.
It beckons me for a midnight dance.
As I bask in the glory of this beautiful orb,
Like an enchanted princess in a castle's tower.
Waiting for my prince hour by hour.
I throw my hands out and ask the moon *Why?*
I waited patiently for the moon's reply.
"My Child" the moon said to me.
"If you slow down and not go so fast, things will improve. . .
Let go of the past!"

Sharon A. Valen
Bakersfield, CA

Circle Box

We live inside a circle sphere,
where curses are the thing I hear.
Where the limit is the ceiling sky,
and I curl my wings; no space to fly.

But in my mind's a box, a square,
clean cut edges of no despair.
Where I can see every fading moment,
and have no fear of dead atonement.

Gabriella S. Morace
Philadelphia, PA

Autumn Breeze

Everyone has it;
a weak spot
that if even a stranger was to reach for,
their entire world could collapse like dominoes.
Not a single person is blessed with a single burden;
they come in packages.
Packages I'm staring at as I sit here in the train station;
with a ticket for no destination.
They all look so different:
in size, color, and content.
How deceiving,
everyone is the same.
We just have schemas—boxes in our heads—
some are more full than others.
It's the subjectivity of reality.
Make excuses all you want.
Continue to allow what is of your control
to be blamed on the fingerprints of another.
To allow misfortune to bog you down
is facile as breathing.
Put forth the extra energy
and break the bonds of calamity.
Only you can set yourself free.

Hope C. McDevitt-Labatt
Arlington, VT

For Those Who Fear

In a cloudy far, far away town,
There rested barren ground.
No one was around.
Yet in that ground there lived a seed so tiny no one could see;
And all that seed wanted was to be a tree.
It was a little lost and didn't know what was to become,
But one miraculous day, the clouds pulled away,
And the little seed looked up and saw the sun.
From that day on little by little it fought its crusty shell
Until it arose on that forgotten land
In which it began to dwell.
Years went by and through the sunshine and the rain,
The seed's wish came true for it became a tree.
But it wasn't like any other tree it wasn't stout or plain;
It grew so high and its trunk intertwined, filling it with life.
It could not have been that way if it had not been for strife.
As the sun watched from up above she couldn't help but beam
For out of all the other things in the world
This is the best she had seen.
On its leaves beautiful petals grew,
Which attached were seeds and on the wind they swirled.
So from this one special tree spewed
Hope for the rest of the world.

Jennifer S. Branch
Jamison, PA

For Tommy: A special friend and an important part of my life. With his bright mind
and loving spirit I have incredible faith he will sprout into the most beautiful tree of all.

Windows Galloping

Stallion strong eyes saw through
as if I were windows waiting grime
old judgment now seem young
and rather yearling of me
as I then suckled away old ego's tit,
where as now my mare holds strong,
now my mare sees through your stallion strong eyes.
And on this 3rd try a thoroughbred intention pried
because perseverance paid,
because your cream window washers
climbed up scaffold water towers high.
And now higher trots and tobacco
by fire light smolders
and tin cans clink food made in mountains
with stallion strong beside.

Trish L. Waters
Haleiwa, HI

The Joke Man

There was a man who jokes every day.
It was me,
It is not me.

Sometimes,
He became a doctor,
But also he becomes a poor writer.

When he is a writer,
He envies the good thing to do,
So he is a doctor again.

He tells a joke as he is a doctor.
He doesn't know after all that
He was a forever writer.

Philip I. Shin
Los Angeles, CA

The Only One Left to Hurt Me, Is Me

I just can't seem to understand why I deserve all this pain and
    heartache.
I guess this is the way it's supposed to be.
I was looking for love and I got it.
I remember the days that I was so eager to satisfy you,
I got hurt and bruised just to prove that I could walk beside you.
I love you with all my heart and I don't know why you did what you did.
I just wanted you to grab me and tell me that I meant something to you.
I thought of death how it would stop if I did.
If only you had let me go, I'd be the one feeling sorry.
I can't believe that was that and it just ended.
I just wanted to be special, I've had so much belief in you
and I wanted to believe that I'm what makes you the best.
But I guess I'm just another female in line.
I always wanted you to be happy, loved the times when you would
    just grab me
look at me with those sparkles in your eyes
like I'm part of the reason why you felt the way you did.
I always thought of you as the best and treated you like a king
just wishing and hoping that I would be your queen.
I never listened to all the gossip, I tried to give you all that you wanted.
If you wanted a doormat to step on and spit on I would be one.
You just looked at me and said that it was all my fault.
I loved you so much that I would forget.
Before I met you I was looking for love.
It's probably the reason it ended messed up.
I'm not looking for love never again.
The only one left to hurt me, is me.

Josephine Hooper
Tununak, AK

Rebirth

8000 days I live this life,
and in the last pages of one chapter,
so begins another.
From the known to the unknown I enter.
Resetting my mind that's been filled with dos and don'ts.
Rights and wrongs.
Truths and lies.
Illusions and fears.
Releasing myself from habitual thinking,
I float down the river of a thousand sensations.
The final frontier stares back into my eyes
as a mirror image of my true potential.
So begins the climactic battle of the spiritual warrior within.
Overcoming all odds.
So love may rule all.
Once again.

Michael A. Bannister
Phoenix, AZ

Traveling the world shines light on how different cultures share many similarities. We all seek something. Reflecting on my life's experiences, I began to ask what it was that I was searching for. In time, I saw that everyone I have met and shared words with was in some way telling me something. They all whispered the silent language of love and set an example of what to do and how to live, thus the poem was inspired to give what I had received.

The Playground

I hope that we go to the playground today.
I really just want to go there and play.
I know that if I try to be good
and pick up my toys the way that I should,
eat all of my pancakes and get dressed real fast,
My mommy and daddy will take me at last.
My little brother Alex can go with us too
and sit in his stroller and play peek-a-boo.
I will swing on the swings and slide on the slide,
then jump on the merry-go-round for a glide.
I will do it all over again and again
and stay for as long as I possibly can.
And when mommy tells me it is time to leave,
I will cry and ask her, "Just one more time please?"
She will give me that chance if I will be good
and eat all my lunch the way that I should.
I will run to the slide and come down it real fast,
I always love to do that one last.
Then we'll walk home together, my family and I,
I'll eat all my lunch or at least I will try.
I will crawl up on my daddy's lap, I will be sleepy,
It's time for a nap.
But tomorrow maybe we'll go there again
and maybe tomorrow
I'll meet a new friend.

Brenda A. Monroe
Bridgeport, WV

I grew up in Bath, Main. I spent twenty-three years as a U.S. Navy wife and my husband Jennings and I now reside in Bridgeport, West Virginia. My poetry is inspired by fond memories of my childhood, but mostly by my children, Robert, Terra, Nixon, and Katelynn. Also by my grandchildren, Izabella, Alex, Morgan, Trent, and Morrison. This particular poem was written for my granddaughter Izabella who loves going to the park to play and would often talk to me about wanting to make new friends.

My Pain

I stand in the rain
as they feel my pain.
I'm not a ghost.
I wont be the host.
As I get poured on
everyone is still gone .
No one seems to care,
as I stand there and begin to bare.
I'm not weak
nor shy to speak.
They start to glare
now but don't spare
I stand there
and begin to tear
everything in my path.
It's like I'm taking a bath.
This way I won't stay
or I won't get my way.
I'm still as a house
but stuffed as a mouse.

Shakeysha D. M. Collins
Chicago, IL

Living Gems

One's life is like a precious gemstone.
One can only see the facets after a cutting job.
This could involve merely tumbling amidst and against other gems
But the stone shines brightly from abrasive forces.
Those gems without sheen must be the rocks who lie dormant, never
butting against another, consequently, never feeling.
Growth happens with buffeting.
Learning occurs from the experience of conflict and
Empathy occurs from like situations.
Oft times, the deeper the cut,
the more dazzling the interior of one's soul.
So brightly shines experience that others recognize the beauty
as it cracks through a rough, crude exterior and
lights the world with understanding.
Pain can be a winning force if a person chooses to accept
suffering as lessons for betterment.
Rounding off the sharp edges is done by spiritual
closeness to like stones.

Gwen A. Zoch
Mountain Home, AR

When I Die

Tears streamed down my face when I saw you that way.
I love you, Grandpa, I will love you every day.
As my tears raced down my face,
I knew you'd soon be in a happier place.
My love will follow you wherever you go.
Oh how I loved you so.
Although I feel sorrow and hate,
You can't fight fate.
You told me everything as time passed by and by.
I never wanted you to die.
We did a lot together throughout the years.
It's time to wipe away the tears.
I want you to know
I will never let you go.
I know you loved me, too.
My heart will always be with you.
Now it's time to say goodbye
Until I see you again someday when I die.

Katrina D. Wood
Bloomingdale, IN

13 Kisses

Almost 13 years ago
I went up to my mother
And asked her for a little baby sister or a brother

I promised to take care of it
Every day and night
And even on the chances that we get into a fight

And when you came into my Life
I wasn't sure what to think.
Seems like only yesterday
You wore pigtails and pink

You're growing up so fast
It makes me wanna cry
from the way we laugh at things
or dance when water falls from the sky

Almost 13 years ago,
I asked God for a friend
One that's smart and beautiful
and loving to no end

but Instead I got something better
Instead I got a girl
One with pretty brown hair
One that danced and twirled

She's different from the other
The kids from other misters
She has a lot of names
But the best one is
My sister

Kaylee R. Flores
Corona, CA

Denial's Vengeance

Denial, denial.
The truth in disguise.

He festers
And itches
Beneath all the lies.

A friendship.
A courtship.
A feeling.
Suppressed.

You want it.
You need it.
But never confess.

Confession, confession.
Revenge of the truth.
He will have his vengeance
Beginning with you.

And when you've been finished,
I'll bow to my knees.
And truth will find justice
Finishing me.

Nicole A. Stetz
Dannemora, NY

Let It Go

Let it go like the wind wisping through trees.
Let it go like a leaf in the winter cold breeze.
Let it go like a flower sending off seeds.
Let it go like the sun giving off beams.
Let it go like a secret left untold.
Let it go like paper left for you to unfold.
In life there are a lot of things to let go of,
but there are more things to hold onto and love.

Diana B. Taylor
Chesterfield, VA

Raised to Fear the Everything

The end draws near,
try and fight the cheer,
soon to be displaced,
with bold fits of change,
and in that aftermath,
I am driven to invent,
a new life,
where dreams breathe,
and I again greet death,
and never again cower,
as a shivering fool,
raised to fear the everything.

Jonathan L. Word
Lakewood, WA

White Man's Puppet

You have strings on your arms and a stick up your ass,
But tell me black man how long will it last?
Not for long like the sand at the top of the hour glass.
You curse us like them, to their racist jokes you laugh,
Like an ignorant educated fool who forgot his past.
You were put there for a reason, to help us get there too;
Not to put us down and brag to your new found crew,
That white man, your idol with his eyes of blue.
But not all white men are the same as he;
Who made us struggle and can't stand to see
Us equal, side by side with a better society.
They made you hate us and love them and their laws you obey;
They brainwashed you and coach the words that you say,
To your family, your brothers, your sisters day after day.
To me you're still in slavery, but there're no chains this time, instead;
There're no whips; you're not imprisoned,
But you're locked down in your head.
So break those strings you white man's puppet!
Look what you've become.
And use where you are to help others like you and me.

Anthony D. Thomas
Santa Ana, CA

Not Asleep

Picking up where we left off among the stains and stable troughs my
    hand becomes a path into my veins
And if I manage to shake off this dredge in which I walked across
    the longest bridge and toppled off like rain
But saints and saintly sinners cracking smiles and pointing fingers
    washing stains from the windows painted red
Will try but quickly failing, to stay awake I'm sailing out this waking
    nightmare aching twitching bed
My shadow has a name and a stately white horse figure clutch me
    closely breathe your gold inside of me
For if I fall profusely, make sure to not refuse me one more wisping
    float atop the sparkling sea
And all the times I scream and shout inside my head not coming out
    my mouth the way it crawled across my eyes
And every time that I want out each door beside me spewing grout
    reminds me that this hallway's a disguise
So lying here my belly aches grinding false bicuspids shake my head
    falls off and rolls under this bed
Leaning sideways looking round I notice that this filthy ground is no
    more less or more than what's been said
So everything is every thing and all the things are everything and
    everything but nothing will delude
And so my time spent rummaging in others' rooms beneath their feet
    they never woke and here I must conclude

Ian R. Phillips
Bloomfield Hills, MI

The March

Daddy said he loved me as he held my hand. He told me to always remember my family and never forget who I am. I said, I will never forget Daddy.

He smiled at me and we walked.

Mommy said she loved me as she moved a stray hair from my head. She told me to be brave and always look for goodness and never forget to forgive. I said, I will never forget Mommy.

She smiled at me and we walked.

They died that day, on that walk. But I never forgot. I never forgot.

I looked up at the sky and smiled as I walked.

Carol F. Ehrenreich
Chambersburg, PA

Slowly Weeping

It's almost tech time
Now it is half past nine
Every day I walk in fear
In hopes that the bully is not near

I look around at all the crowns
Hoping she does not come out of bounds
Suddenly I see her in the corner
Following me around the border

She's almost catching up to me
Hoping that I have time to flee
She grabs me by my shirt with glee
Sad that's all she thinks of me

She threw me inside her locker
I think she is kind of bonkers
I feel ashamed to show my face
Because I flow in a very slow pace

I'm at home at last to try to sleep
But instead I start to weep
Morning comes at a blink of an eye
But instead of saying hi I say bye

Hannah A. Dymond
Bronx, NY

Is It Forever?

Is it forever,
Or are we a fire
that slowly dies with time?
Or ice that melts away,
In the heat of the day?

Forever is it really true?
Is it some desire we are born with,
That we will crave 'til death?
Or is forever a myth?

Isn't the sun forever,
Or the sea?
If the sky goes on forever,
Then why can't we?

We are brighter than fire,
And give off more light!
We are stronger than ice,
And for you I will fight.

Forever... it must be true!
'Cause I can't imagine living forever...
Without you!

Sara L. Gray
Beatty, NV

Monster Inside

I stare at the face across from me
the face of a liar and thief
I want to obliterate the face with my fists
A little smirk appears on the face and angers me further
The face just stares at me with its green eyes
I can't take it anymore and as I move to strike
a light goes off in my head it's a mirror

Shawn E. Boner
Burlingame, KS

the end

is this how we are to end?
after all the time we did spend?
can you honestly say
this is how you want it to stay?
your silence is killing me
is this really how you want it to be?
i can't take anymore
can't hang on like before
if i go before you're back hon
please tell me what i have done
this is how we end
goodbye dear friend

Darlene H. Proper
Saratoga Springs, NY

Stand

Lord, I love You,
I know that this is true,
Others turn against me,
Because I do what You want me to!

Before I was running from You,
Trying to please Man,
Today I run to You
So that I will be able to stand!

When the enemy has camped all around me,
Pressuring me time after time,
You always say, "Toni, be strong;
I'll lend you a helping hand,"
That's why, dear Lord, I am able to stand!

Misfortunes come and yes they go,
But why do they not pass me by?
"Because Toni, when opportunity knocks,
you always turn and run!"

"Don't be afraid and don't look back,
Burn the bridges you cross,
For that—that you never had,
Is that—that can never be lost!

Toni W. Johnson
Berry, AL

I live in Fayette County, Alabama. In 1994 I was diagnosed with bipolar disorder. I struggled with mania for many years. After being hospitalized in 2004, a doctor prescribed medication that has kept my disorder under control. I attended a Woman Thou Art Loosed conference in 1999 in Atlanta, Georgia. Afterwards, I realized I had a special gift for writing inspirational and motivational poetry. During phases of my mania is when my creativity for writing skyrockets. I have been married for eighteen years and we have three wonderful children and one grandson.

Uh Oh, I Lost My Personality

Charismatic way of life
You pull, you peel, but ignore the advice
Dig in deep to hide the grievance
Pain is prettiest when drenched in credence
Hold your head up while spitting out gloom
Hypocrisy hits hardest when you enter the room

Sit me down, feed me stolen thoughts
Your fake way of living makes me wet and hot
Conforming with nonconformists is all the rage
Name off the Gods you've heard, but half were never engaged
The coffee shop and you will be my doom
Hypocrisy hits hardest when you enter the room

Tana M. Cox
Denham Springs, LA

Forgotten

If days turned to hours I would have to devour the bittersweet and sour
candy apple kisses that decorate my wish list every time we create this
dream that's everlasting, nothing's worth more than having, piece of
heaven grabbing
Ineffable experience, that makes me wanna clench my fist in
orgasmic tortuous bliss.

If I could undoubtably find the thread of a line that intertwines our
love so divine
that the birds stop singing, bells stop ringing, and dreamers stop believing
that the sun rises on her smile and addicts finally admit denial, then
you may put my love on trial, 'cause then I'll
prove to you and tell you why, love is rope that may never be untied,
burned down nor denied.

If ice turned to crystals, lingering kisses under the mistletoe while
the wind whistles
behind my ear while I'm standing here tellin' you baby come near
the fire where the flames do burn and our desires may take a
dangerous turn
into the thoughts of what we ought not, but somehow in the moment
forgot.

Tarletta S. Williams
Tallahassee, FL

Ink

I am a warrior of ink!
My pen and words are my weapon.
With them I can create worlds
and take you to places you will never see.
I can create power or subtlety,
I can fashion and destroy
imagery of the utmost elegance.
I am the god of this world upon paper.
Everything I create, I could just
as easily destroy with a single
flick of words. I am a warrior
of Ink!

Wesley L. Coker
Gainesville, FL

The Black Woman

I am brown though the name you gave me is black
I gave long braided hair and a strong back
full figured from my lips down to my hips
I am not categorized by my skin color or my gender
but by my strength behind the list of great African-American leaders
Was a strong black woman yet soothing and soft hearted
the heart of her African man
Her warmth draws from the sun soothing his soul
Her smile drowns all his sorrows back into the darkness
She's the healer; she's love and grace
All possibilities are seen only through her eyes, the black woman

Kamarin F. Hubbard
Union, OH

Unbreakable

If just one heart were unbreakable,
Oh Lord, let it be mine
Because I'm tired of having it ripped from my sleeve
I'm tired of spending my nights crying
The perfect moments aren't worth having
Because eventually they come to an end
And all you're left with are memories
Of times you'll never experience again
If just one person were made perfect
Dear God, let me be that one
The loves I lost, I wouldn't have
And the lonely nights would be done
I wouldn't be replaced with one more beautiful
I wouldn't be left alone
And my heart would take permanent residence
And no longer have to roam
This is one of those moments that aren't worth having
One that has to end
So I'm trying to fight the laws of time
But it seems I just cannot win
I wish I were invincible!
Blessed with an unbreakable heart
Because slowly but surely I see you fading
I know this is the part where the end starts

April A. James
Lithonia, GA

Brown Man

A brown man has stepped in to the highest office in the land.
While chanting these words, "Yes, we can." He walked up the steps
built by slavery hands,
Again saying, "Yes, we can."
Some of us do not understand, but we know we trust this brown man
that has liberated us from the master's hand.
Never will we see the plantation again.
Never will we be beaten again.
Never will our brothers be lynched again.
The Brown Man has climbed the mountain that could not be climbed.
He has reached the highest of high.
He has made the old and the young cry.
He has completed the path began by so many who have died.
He will bring us together across all of the land because now we
believe these words:
"Yes, we can."

Orlando A. Vivians
Waterloo, IA

Marcie's Fifth Birthday

"Today is my birthday and I got new shoes!" said Marcie,
as she danced down the street in her brand new shoes,
because she just turned five and what else was she to do?
She met a little girl standing all alone and she said,
"My name is Marcie. What is yours?"
"My name's Tracy and I am four."
Marcie said, "You want to play?"
Tracy said, "I can play all day. My mommy said so, yes she did.
My mommy says I should learn to play,
'cause she said I will grow strong that way.
"My mommy," said Marcie,"said that I'm growing like a weed,
not really a weed, but like a weed.
Today's my birthday and I got new shoes.
My mommy says we're going to the zoo. Want to come along?"
"Oh, yes! I really do. I'll ask my mommy, maybe she'll come too."
"My daddy," said Marcie, "He'll buy ice cream and candy on a stick
and if you come too, I'll share some with you.
We'll be friends forever, that's what we'll do.
I've got to go home now, we'll be back at two
and don't forget we're going to the zoo.
Tell your mommy not to be late, 'cause this is a very important day.
It's my birthday and I got new shoes,
I got new shoes and I'm going to the zoo, and now I've met you.
Oh, what a birthday this is going to be.
I'm going to remember this day for the rest of my life. I will. I will.
Wheeeee!"

Mary L. Armbruster
Hollister, CA

Poetry Is...

Poetry is a snowflake drifting to the floor.
Poetry is a closed and opened door.

Poetry is my heart, core and much, much more.
Poetry is a teardrop falling,
And a dream calling.

Poetry is a flower blooming in barren ground.
Poetry is a howling blood hound.

Poetry is my best friend.
A new beginning but never an end.

Poetry is anything and everything.

Anna M. Nappo
Littleton, CO

Apathy Destroys Empathy

I see the troubles that no one else does.
I smell the rotting beneath the peach fuzz.
Only I do, it is my cross to bear.
But I am no Christ, don't put me up there.
I am gifted with vision, but do I take cause?
No! I sit and I sulk and I twiddle my paws.
The trouble resides as a thorn in my brain,
And slowly my apathy drives me insane.

Timothy M. Condon
Denver, CO

I Want To

I want to go back,
Back to where neither of us hurt one another.
To where our love wasn't bruised by ignorance,
But instead sheltered by our warm embrace.
Where every day felt like a dream not a tragedy.
Where our feelings ran rampant,not shuttered in fear.
Where the slightest touch sent chills down our spines,
not splinters to our hearts.
Where tears fell 'cause of the love we felt eternally, not involuntary.
Can we start anew and reject the thorns that ripped us deep,
and ignite the flame that burned with so much heat?

Tiffany N. Baez
Winter Springs, FL

I Am an Artist

I am a artist when I sketch a picture.
I am a artist when I forget everything that
happened and go with the flow.
I am a artist when I draw a world that
is in my head and don't care about how people judge me.
I am a artist when I pick up a pad and
draw what I feel inside of me.
I understand people are afraid that
they will get picked on because they
show their true colors.
I might get picked on but at least
I am not afraid of it.

Angelina S. Murphy
Albany, NY

A True Fairy Tale

David planned a story book wedding a few months in advance,
A surprise for Jennifer, filled with romance.
Without knowing what size that she might wear,
Her rings and her dress were bought with a guess and a prayer.
All travel and hotel reservations to Lake Tahoe were made,
Jennifer thought she was just going on another skiing escapade.
They left Thursday morning, their parents left Thursday night,
Arriving in Reno on two separate flights.
He planned to propose on the snowy ski slopes,
She would answer him with a "yes," or so he hopes.
At the base of the mountain in the Hershey's Chocolate Shop,
David placed a ring on her finger, and the question he did pop.
Overwhelmed she began to cry, her face pressed against his chest,
He held her ever so tightly, then softly asked, "Does this mean yes?"
"Of course it is a Yes!" Through her tears of joy she replied,
"I wish Mom and Dad were here," she said, as they stepped outside.
As they walked hand in hand to the prearranged rendezvous,
When she sees our parents, David wondered, what will she do?
"David, that woman looks like my mom," she said rather calm.
"It is my Mom! And my Dad! And your Dad! And your Mom!"
There were lots of hugs and kisses, giggles and grins.
"You've got to be kidding me!" she exclaimed again and again.
Her dad began to tell about having to carry the dress . . .
"Wait! The Dress?! Am I getting married?" The answer was yes.
Exchanging promises before family and God therewith,
Now they were Mr. and Mrs. Smith.

Brenda L. Stanley
Freeport, TX

Love to Make It Bloom

Everything's blooming
But not as it should
Your voice is what kept them in bloom

Though it pains me to say
You're no longer here to tend to the roses
that awaken with fear
the lilies are now looking silly
the daisies look awfully hazy
the vines now intertwine with crooked lines

Nothing is growing right
What should I do?

You're no longer here to keep me from wilting.

…you're no longer here
To make me bloom.

Nancy A. Pedraza
Fontana, CA

The Rapid Sands of Time

When I sat down at the kitchen table
I began to write a poem about love at first sight
I could not help myself but to stop and stair at the hourglass
which was given unto thee the chance to spend the time
with my ladylove before the day she would pass.
I would sit there hour after hour,
looking at the hourglass
wondering, will I have enough time left to spend the last day
with her on the purified white clouds of romance?
Whenever I look at the purified rapid sand inside of the hour glass
I get sad and very emotional
because it was time for my baby girl to depart
away from thee. I get sad and very emotional
because it was time for my baby girl to silently depart away
from me now when I was about to give her that sweet long
but too late waited proposal.

Phillip S. Berrian
Valdosta, GA

A Lovely Past

For years you have caused pain,
For years you have destroyed.
You make it rain,
You tortured me as your toy.

Years have passed,
I yearn to let go of the past.
You bring it up,
It has become like an overfilled cup.
It overflows,
With tears of my sorrows.

You move on
without conscience.
While I stay behind
to deal with the consequence.

I sit here in pain,
While you are oblivious.
You leave these problems for me to drain,
While you think I am tedious.
I struggle to rise above
all of this pain you so dearly love.

Sherri N. Warren
Wasilla, AK

For My Sister

When we were young, I can remember
you saying you wanted to be
pretty like me.
When we were young, I can remember
you saying, "I want to be
just like you."
When we were young, I can remember
you saying sweetly, "I Love You," and
telling me you needed me.
When we were young, I can remember
how I let you down.
Now that we are older, I hope you can see
how much more beautiful you always were
than me.
Now that we are older, I am happy to see
that you turned out nothing like me,
for you are far more perfect than I could
ever be.
Now that we are older, I hope you see
how I want to be that sister
you needed me to be.
Now that we are older, I hope you see
just how special you are to me.
Now that you are grown, I hope you believe
that I love you baby girl; you mean
the world to me!

Barbara A. Langston
Danielsville, GA

All That's Left of Me

I turned to look at him.
I could see in his eyes.
The walls were built again,
not his, but mine.

I've gone away from him again,
one piece at a time.
Shielding my feelings.
Searching my mind.

I'm not myself with him,
afraid of who I am.
Because I don't even know,
and he'll not understand.

To shut him out is a reflex,
quick as a tap on the knee.
I hide myself away,
all that's left of me.

Wendy L. Balcerowski
Mayville, WI

Bounce

The human spirit is perennial as the grass
in the face of disenchantment, we shall bounce.
The dimensions withstand moments of time
As new discoveries are revealed.

Ambiguity still lingers with strong, blowing presence
Forcing us to look; the wonderment will prevail
Grace and dignity be chariot sisters riding gently
Each day shall unfold as the universe suggests.

Believing in all that is righteous and rare
resilience abounds in gentle minds, wistful souls.
Linger in the warmth of the sunlight today
Contentment desired; obtain it with honor.

Ultimate surrender transcends who we are
harmony translates our knowing to peace.
Judgments replaced by mindful, generous love
Society returning to the fundamentals of humanity.

Faith is individual, mixed beliefs must hold hands
Aspiration and hope speak one language
of definition and character demanding a change.
Our children's tomorrows belong to us today.

I wish these ideals to be air that we breathe
yet I fear that humanity combined is dispirited.
Succumb not to its illumination of discontent
Truth be to self, strength be our guide as we
escort those in need of the bounce.

Monica R. Greer
Des Moines, IA

For Mum (I Miss You)

Feels like another lifetime,
that is, since you were here.
Not a phone call or a visit,
and it's only been two years.

It's a constant re-adjustment,
every time the seasons change.
Now the only way to get close to you
is by going to your grave.

I have wanted so badly
to dig down into the earth
with my bare hands to hold
the one who gave me birth.

I wait, watch, and listen
with the utmost of care,
just in case you say or do something
while I am there.

But it's another disappointment,
as no miracles take place.
Spend the rest of my day
wiping tears from my face.

Erin E. Nichols
Hampton Falls, NH

This poem is extremely personal to me. It is a reflection of the feelings I experience while visiting my mother's grave. It's seldom a positive endeavor, as I always leave there more upset than I had been prior to arriving. I wrote this poem while I was going through a difficult situation and yearned for the guidance, love, and support only she could provide. It was a time I needed to express myself. I was not concerned with proper poetic form or grammar; I simply needed to get the emotions I was experiencing off my chest.

Nobody

What I do I've done but have not yet learned the reason God has
sent me. Why do I respect my foolish ways? *Why must I repent on
Jesus*...and not those trying to tempt me? Who will protect me? For
if I defy the Lord and do not love or respect myself, who will love or
respect me? *Nobody.* Look at me now, look at where I've led myself.
I've landed in the same exact place that I've landed repeatedly, only
now I'm alone, I am afraid. For there is no more shoulder to lean
on or bridge to cross. I am lost, Jesus; help me. I know I've asked
you numerous times, but I never knew it would come down to this.
Besides you, Lord, who is there to help me through this? *Nobody.*
I've burnt my last bridge, I've crushed my only dream, and that
dream was to make my family proud. But where is my family? For
I am now most disappointed in myself. I've failed me, I'm a loser.
Everything they said would happen came true. I'm a loser. I was
wrong and they were right. Now who's with me on these sad and
lonely nights? *Nobody.* At first it was nothing, a fluke, a mishap. I
would joke and laugh. I would fight and steal, not knowing that this
nightmare which I was warned of was real...real indeed. It went
from a dream to life. Did everyone leave me? No, it was me. I left
them no choice but to move on and let go. I'm my own worst enemy.
Besides myself, who was there to fear? *Nobody.* Now as I sit here
with me and my thoughts, all that's left is hope. I hope I change. I
hope I succeed. I hope I make it through this desperate time of need.
Yet, I hope I die, I hope I decease, I hope I don't wake up and that
God will take me in my sleep. I feel the devil's got me, but not for
long. I still hope there is hope for me in this world, because without
my son, I'm *nobody*. He's my number one in life and second without
myself, I'm *nobody*.

Daniel Ray Hickman
Elizabeth, WV

Australian Sunrise

The seed
    The synthetic
The thought
    The dream
The need
    The lie
The act
    The power
The destruction
    The absolute
The past
    The pain
The truth
    The survival
The revival
    The love
The idea
    The will
To dream past the love. . .

Linda Givens
Smyrna, GA

Starlight

You're like a star.

I was attracted to your light, and allured by your gravity. I was captured by your beauty.

Now I move, always in circles, knowing that one day I will be consumed by you.

I am not afraid, for your fire is ecstasy.

James V. Powers
Dallas, TX

Flying

I wish I could fly
High up in the sky.
Over the horizon,
Just as the sun has risen.
Using all my might
To fly 'til night,
I will float like a kite
With only a few respites
Until the moon is lit.
Up in the air like an eagle,
I am the only one able.
A poignant experience it shall be,
The first flying human being…me!

Lucia Zhang
Sugar Land, TX

The Liquid of Life

Love is water,
the well that bubbles over.
The liquid that is missing
in a land so far away.

The water in our body
sustains us, empowers us.
We crave the need
to wet our tongue.

If we choose to go without
we will not endure
because water is love
and love is water

Sigrid C. Derickson
Atascadero, CA

I am fifteen years old and a freshman in high school. I enjoy gardening and reading. I am in the marching and wind ensemble bands where I play the tuba. I love to write fiction and create awesome stop motion videos. The inspiration for this poem came from an avocado seed resting, half-submerged, in a cup of water on the windowsill. It was inspirational because the avocado could not live without the water and the water was just water without the avocado pit.

Perfect

Alone by a cliff side, a young boy lurks.
He is interested. Not in the beautiful nature or the breeze, but in what lies beyond...He looks in four ways...Behind him, to his left, to his right, and over the edge of the cliff. There seems to be promise for him only in one direction...

A perfect feeling, but in all honesty, what are the chances of it lasting?

A young girl's heart pounds with what seems to be everlasting joy. She has found "the one"...her love. Her knight in shining armor. Her silver lining. She embraces every flawless aspect of him, knowing that her heart is now held by two different spirits. And as gentle as the calmest ocean, she sighs in infinite admiration.

A perfect feeling, but in all honesty, what are the chances of it lasting?

A sprinter with everything on the line: his career, his family, his values, and his life, races for the last time.
He pushes himself, and with each footstep, visions of his past and his future alternate in true harmony. As he comes foot-to-foot with the 1st place runner, everything prior to that moment...is unnecessary... Home stretch, 10 yards to go, neck-and-neck, and...

Photo finish. The runner, victorious in much more than the competition, sheds tears of complete pride and joy.

A perfect feeling, but in all honesty, what are the chances of it lasting?

"Perfect" is never promised. "Perfect" is perilous. "Perfect" is perceived, but is never proven. "Perfect" is a psychological problem.

If any being is unlucky enough to meet "perfect" face-to-face, they'll immediately come to find...that perfect...is an imperfection.

Taqi A. Mustafaa
Cedar Hill, TX

Free One Day

We live in the ghetto or to some a concentration camp
Much is to despair living here
A cry is heard from the shower shack above
"Mom!" he yells then his cry calms down
What is to become of us? Will we one day again be free?
Are there possibilities to trust again?
How can these men and women in uniform be so cruel and not feel a
　　bit of sadness
"For their hearts are so stiff," one said, "they don't carry the feeling
　　to let pain and sorrow in."
Cold all day, below freezing at night: no blankets, no stories to read
　　to young children tonight.
"On your feet," a soldier said with a rip-roaring yell, "We march
　　through the night till you weep and yell!"
So tired and weak, barely holding a heartbeat
　Can we keep living or is our life about to end?
"No," I said, "Keep going. You can do it; have faith in yourself for
　　you will pull through it."
Scurrying for food that is thrown to us while the soldiers stood in
　　front laughing at us
Eating so fast not even making a sound,
Closing my eyes to forget the place that I am in,
Gun fire.
Many yell and we all turn.
A man comes and stands in front of us;
He yells, "You are free, you are free."

Tatiana Laurance
Puyallup, WA

Humanity

To love or to leave?
To be open and believe,
That people mean well and are not immersed in pride, control and
  hypocrisy.
Or do we choose to be frightened and hesitate,
Or to be vulnerable and isolate?
In response to human nature's tend to hate; to point, to burn, to
  humiliate.
To rejoice in others' anguish, failings, self-loathing, and pain
To scrutinize and stare at the demise and shame
Of others rather than ourselves.
To rather dig within and identify our own wounds,
Our own fears, resentments, and hidden cries.
We are human and have such things, it's our commonality as human
  beings.
The wounds you carry and choose today
Can be healed if only worked on and identified.
We can become together, a better community
People united in growth and unity
Able to love, communicate, and share
Our talents, our thoughts, and together bring
A loving world both from our reality and hidden dreams.
So what shall be your choice?
To accept and bring forth our caring compassion
Our enduring sense of hope?
Or shall you choose to chase
After pride, power, and becoming the master.
For the only result these things shall bring,
Are injustice & empowered anarchy.

Nancy S. Mattos
San Jose, CA

Destruction

A perfect field of white,
Undisturbed by black lines,
Sits on the desk before me.

A pen sits in my hand,
Ready to start writing.
But my thoughts are not so pretty.

They cannot fill this page
With wisdom in each word,
The way I wish I could write.

Besides, it is perfect.
Who would destroy this page
With some pointless, broken words?

Braden J. Mauldin-Heiner
Coeur d'Alene, ID

D.A.R

The realist
Death and rebirth of Shawnta Blue
Fighting every day of my past present and future
Deciding if I'm a child of God or the son of Lucifer
Bitter feeling of people questioning my judgment of life
From my oldest daughter, mother, to my ex-wife
From the problems with my mother or the growing pains I have for
    my brother
From the love I have for my job and dedication
For the love I have for the alcohol I consider my medication
From the keeping it real moments in life and the slits in my arm I cut
    with that knife
From the lies about my father that came to the light
And even though he's gone I still deal with that fight
I've come a long way with the battles of my demons
From now then even from my father's semen
I was and am a good-hearted, strong-hearted person so bold
But sometimes bleeding hearts turn cold
I'm not being different as what you would say
I'm not living for you no more; it's for me I will stay
My priorities are in order, I'm focused and true
This is the death and rebirth of *Shawnta Blue*

Shawnta M. Blue
Antioch, TN

Another Day

Each morning as the sun rises
My eternal bliss vaporizes

Then I visualize you there
And it appears that
It was always here

As the warmth from sleep dissipates
You follow

As the day grovels
Your image lingers on
And waits to only be had again

Upon retiring the day
You are slow to leave
Only to come another day

Relentless to my mind
Forever hoping you will be mine

Nick J. Pasternak
Joliet, IL

The Tiny Flower

Swaying in the gentle breeze, feeling the whizzing noise of the meadows
I longed to hasten my blooming moment, then remembered,
"patience is a virtue"
There is an order for everything, I need to wait for the time
predestined by the Mighty Power
Then it happened....slowly slithering through the spread out green sepals
I looked at the light, "Thank you Sun," for the energy you gave us to
sprout and bloom
Looking at myself for the first time I saw the eye-catching color of
my body, no painter can match
Feeling my body, the softness so sensual I blushed
"Oh My God! I am pretty, I am beautiful"
Then I turned in the gentle breeze, looked around in the meadow
"Oh My!" I exclaimed
What a sight! Rainbow of colors: Purple, Yellow, Violet, Green
Flowers they are
Like myself but so much more beautiful and colorful,
so many more different sizes and shapes
Carpeting the world around me belittling my Ego
I sensed a swift movement in my body, looked up,
saw a creature fluttering the wings so fast
and hovering over smiling at me…gently caressed my inner self
I felt my quivering body succumbing to the bee's desire
gently the pollen of love was transferred...the bee departed
I felt my spirit lifted, for being desirable for someone else
I felt that my being self with the God-given talents, the fragrance and color
I could be useful in a small way to this place where I was born.
Once again the gentle breeze made me dance
and I looked around and learned to synchronize
to be in tune with my fellow beings...all different in shapes & colors
but swaying in the same direction to make the Music of Happiness

Daniel George
Grovetown, GA

I am originally from the southern state of Kerala, India. I came to the United States in
1981. I've lived in Augusta, Georgia for the past thirty years with my wife Gracen and
our children Jibu and Jaya. I am passionate about reading and music. I've written a
few poems in Malayalam, my native tongue. My other interests include travel, reading,
playing tennis, shuttle badminton, and volleyball. I am strongly spiritual and God-
fearing, but I do not see value in denominational/sectarian teachings or philosophies of
any organized religion—especially the ones advocating hatred in the name of a loving
God. Each one of us has talents—use those for the betterment of humanity.

When the World Calls

For when the world calls
Man is challenged to do what is right
Though the continuance of the task is tough
The benefits mold us to our potential

Time and time again will the challenges tear you down
But no challenge is given that man cannot cope with
And when the trial passes
Light beams through and sweeps us from our slumps

Unfortunately the ignorance of the world gets to some
For instead of facing the world
They dash in fear of progress
Fear of change

Fear is nothing but strain
For fear is never needed
We must rise and face the world
For when the world calls man must do what is right

Matthew G. Marlow
Murfreesboro, TN

The Mistake I Met Last Night

Perhaps I had one shot too many,
perhaps loneliness just got the better of me.

I met him twice on the sticky dance floor.
He had the courage that only comes from lager,
mixed with the vodka, ambition.

A country boy, that's what he said
he was.
A drunken one night stand, that's what
I was.

A no-name boy, chiseled into my memory.
A drunken night, a night to be forgotten,
that was anything but
what I expected,
and nothing to satisfy
what I desired.

My only regret...
not knowing his name,
brown eyes, brown curly locks, and just a little facial hair,
enough to make me want him.
My mystery boy.

Tasha N. Hartley
Richfield, PA

The Grumpy Ole' Man

I once stumbled across this man, whose name was "G."
He wanted to remain incognito to protect his privacy.
Such was his nature. His aloofness made him an enigma.
(Is it presumptuous of me to say that the "G" meant grumpiness
or gruffness or even gentleness?)

A grumpy ole' man, fair, but decent, mind you.
Because life dealt him a series of setbacks and despairs,
in which he could not recover to find his aim.
His trademarks: a bottle of brandy, a red handkerchief,
a straw fedora hat, and a pipe.

April. "G" takes his customary strolls, but alone,
through heart and mind and soul, his daily bread.
They see him comin' and flee like rabbits;
I see him comin' and hide within a nearby ole' oak tree;
I see him, but he didn't see me.

"G's" facial expression, a mean and rough one,
an untidy, unshaven black and silver beard.
He treated a smile like it was a cardinal sin,
if, in fact, he ever did smile.

I last saw "G" walk afar off down an old road.
He looked like a dot, out of sight, out of mind.

I am old school; I like sausages and hot cakes.
He is older school. He prefers bacon and eggs and grits.
To be grumpier the next time around, his intent.
And, a grumpy ole' man was he!

Reginald W. Murray
Philadelphia, PA

The Unreachable Face

It's you
You're the unreachable face
The beautiful chime I hear in my sleep
The sunshine kissed hair I long to stroke
On my way to you,
In the hall, on a bus, on a train
the unreachable face
I breathe heavily
Over time,
I could see that you wanted someone else
Feeling foolish and I guess I always knew
Thinking you were meant for me
And I for you
Separated because of waiting
Scared to tell you the truth
How I feel about you
The Unreachable Face

Caley M. Lareau
Cumberland, RI

Teeka, My Little Heartbeat at My Feet

My tear drops fall every night for you,
I keep hoping and praying that this isn't true.
Without you by my side every morning I awake,
Oh dear God this must be some mistake.
Then I remember and feel a rush of pain,
And a blanket of sadness washes over me like the rain,
Teeka's time here was through, You have called her home,
But don't You realize You have left me here all alone?
She was my very best friend,
My most loyal companion,
I still can't believe that this really happened.
Memories of her flood my mind,
Like a tidal wave of pictures during a much happier time.
I love her and miss her so much I can barely breathe.
Why on earth did she have to leave?
She will forever live on in my heart,
Although it'll never be easy for us to be apart.
One day when my time comes and I am called to Heaven,
I will see my Teeka and will kiss her little apple dome head,
And rub her little belly,
Knowing we will be reunited as a family never to be parted again.

Jacqueline E. Twiner
Dumfries, VA

My poem was inspired by my love for a little Chihuahua named Teeka. A Valentine's Day gift from my parents, Teeka came into my life on February 12, 1995. Over the years she provided unconditional love, laughter, and comfort. She was my world, my very best friend. I was blessed to have her in my life for over fifteen years. When that difficult day came that I had to make the decision to put her to sleep, I felt as though a part of me had died. Teeka will forever live on in my heart, and now, this poem.

The Way It Was

There once was a child born from a mother,
Unwanted and unloved, was given to another.
The other was pleased for a moment,
but he was so old and unable
to care for the child of his daughter,
the government stepped in and took her from his table.

From house to house she went, barely able to unpack
the tiny bag she carried on her back.
Tiny and brave with tears in her eyes,
she said no goodbyes.

When life got hard and the pain unbearable,
everything meaningless and the world unstable,
she'd look to the heavens
and pray to the sovereigns.

One day she thought, I'll get out of here
and leave all this behind and be happy, free and clear.
Escape she did, but memories follow,
and a heart can't forget when it's full of sorrow.

Jean M. Martinez
Charlotte, NC

A Sigh

Expulsion of breath, brief release of being
Lending credenced urgency to feeling
Compressing soul's expression with brute force
To pureness of unrefined emotion

Searing pinpricks of heated breath contain
Messages of, as yet, unspoken need
The smallest revelation of true thought
A fault line in the concreteness of heart

Fraught with meaning, brimful of catharsis
Half-restrained desire creeps from parted lips
As impassioned grief or anger breaks free
To quicken Sympathy's warm embraces

Bittersweet savoring of ripened despair
Holds one frail note—before kissing silence.

Maddie E. Myers
Fresno, CA

Death's Bed at Centra State Hospital

Here I sit in Centra State, just like bait, no hook or line nor
tangled twine to confuse the mind, yet still disinclined to
resign my fate. As I lie as if in state, coexisting with time and
faith, in my seemingly meager existence here at Centra State, I'm
eager to discard this persistent pain that flows, flows through
my body like blood through my veins. As if conceding time had run
its course only to be surprised by my beating heart, pumping that
red e-lick-of life in my passive resistance for life as I sit here
in Centra State.
My strife for life seems eons ago, as I lie here waiting for the end,
with my eyes open for the entire world to see, staring as if into
endless space, not a blink, nor a twitch of my nose, it's as if I'm
dangling from a line, as if eternal life is intertwined, no end in
sight, I wonder what's my plight, will it come day or night or not at
all? You see, I hear that here at Centra State, miracles have been
known to placate these gates, there's a chance I might go home.
Yet, my pain I'm not able to communicate, my contrite for not
saying anything prior is evident to those who gaze upon my face,
the agony I've impeded from them all, this look remains upon my
face as I gasp for air, my heart racing, yet faint and more distant,
I silently call out, but they hear me not. Then I see a bright warm
ultraviolet light above my head beckoning me on…
They call my name, but now I'm gone, those standing by my bed
kiss and rub my head, as if to hold me on. I gaze down upon them all.
Yes, I think I've moved on.

Herbert R. Reed
Columbia, SC

Wind Song

The wind speaks in many tones—
An icy blast chills the bones,
A mournful lament amidst the rain,
A soft sigh to ease the pain,
A whisper in the pines above
Gives the promise of summer love.
For dancing flowers, a gentle touch—
The wind speaks and tells us much.

Mary Jean Cimino
Pocasset, MA

The Enemy Within

Hard on me, putting me down;
I won't give up and drown.
If I listen to you, you win.
I've chosen not to hear and myself defend.

I won't live in the jail erected in my mind.
Your harsh words will fail and me not define.
You won't destroy me today.
Helpless, hopeless, and lost is not my way.

Please, leave me be.
You've lost your hold on me.
Myself I've found.
I like me, I'm sticking around.

Yvonne M. Roberts
Elyria, OH

Too Soon Cold

A cold wind shivers across garden's bed,
making flowers wilt under chilly air.
The mums of autumn weep in rusty red
and summer's lawn now sobs in deep despair.

The winter played possum instead of sleep,
its gray lurking frost steals the heat away.
With sheer crystal teeth it begins to creep,
beguiles the yard where leaves refuse to stay,

and pure flakes like cartwheels aren't far behind,
the breeze will growl becoming harsh and fast.
Stars will neglect to shine like night is blind
audacious shadows rob the moon's full cast.

When cold begins to wane and warmth returns
and sun dapples spread a glimmering dress,
slumbering snow with drops and melting learns
to feed the bulbs and seeds that gardens bless.

Marilyn M. Terwilleger
Cheyenne, WY

Having a Determined Mind

Accomplishing great heights
On God's beautiful earth
Remaining steadfast
On this journey quest mission
Placing my heart and soul on paper
God is using me as an instrument
To direct the students
Back to school to gain knowledge
Then going to college you all are the future
God is using me as a vessel to write
For a brighter and safer tomorrow
My faith is deeply rooted in Jesus
He is opening our eyes to the realities of life
Having movers and shakers and every day striving
For a brighter and safer tomorrow
Because knowledge is truly power and power
Will bring upon a change in all of your lives
Shacking those chains and shackles off
One by one for I have decided to dance for Jesus
Oh no devil I have Jesus on my mind
God is molding and shaping my life
To becoming a righteous serious vessel
Having a strong heart and a determined mind
And every day climbing great heights
In order to reach the Promised Land
God is showering his blessing
Straight down from Heaven above
Loving, caring, and giving
Helping one another

Belinda Dorsey
Columbus, GA

Keep Them Safe

When my babies were little and I saw them in danger,
I'd yell back, back, babies get back.
Now they're grown and all alone,
I can't yell back, back, babies get back. My babies are in Iraq.
When my babies were little,
I'd always watch what they were doing.
I'd keep my eyes open and watch for trouble brewing,
I'd yell run, run, run babies run.
Now they're grown and all alone,
I can't yell run, run, run babies run.
My babies are carrying the guns.
When my babies were little,
I'd tell them they could be whatever they wanted to be.
Now they're grown and never alone,
They're being all they can be in the Army.
Who are the boys crawling through the sand?
We are the boys you watched play football from the stands.
Who are the girls carrying the arms?
We are the girls still wearing our sweet 16 charms.
Who are the guys out front shooting the guns?
We are the college guys that had paintball fights for fun.
Who are the girls that are ready to pick up a gun and fight?
We are the young mothers who miss putting their babies to bed at night.
Who are the guys driving the convoys?
We are the fathers who miss playing with our boys.
Who are the girls doing paper work night and day?
We are the girls who miss their mothers so far, far away.
Who are the guys giving out orders?
We are the husbands that miss weekend chores.
Who are the girls out there standing guard?
We are the wives who thought being a housewife was hard.
Who are the troops in that land we do not know?
They are our loved ones and God we miss them so.
And Lord I give them to you each and every one,
Not just my daughter and my son.
I pray you keep them all safe with you until this war is done.

Vivian F. Dietz
Katy, TX

248

Four-Letter Word

When there's discouragement,
put-downs,
and shoves into a dark corner.
When the words
push upon you,
giving you no space to breathe.
When you close your eyes
and tell yourself,
"There is a better world."
He's listening,
listening to every word,
moment,
and countless thought.
He will give you
the strength to breathe again.
To breathe in
what people need most in this world,
a four-letter word:
Hope.

Alex J. Summers
Grangeville, ID

This poem was inspired by my friend's username on this application on my Ipod. This proves that inspiration is found anywhere. My mom didn't even know I submitted this poem until I received this letter. My family supports me and helps me with my spelling. I am terrible at spelling. I'm in the ninth grade and I love to write. Poetry is my hobby and I have so many thoughts to put into poetic form. Some people don't know what talents they have . . . I guess I found mine.

More Than Just a Person

You think you're just a person
Unnoticed and unseen
You'd give anything to be
Just a normal teen

You live a liveable life
Just like all your friends
But you know you're very different
And this is where it ends

But the story still goes on
You live it every day
You lock yourself in silence
'Cause you don't know what to say

But you as well as I
know that that's untrue
You've got a heart of gold
And a mind for speaking too

You're more than just a person
Ever since the start
You'll change the world someday
All 'cause you were set apart

Jayme R. Damm
Trent, SD

Savage Brother

I've got the world in my hands
A master plan,
But I don't know why I keep calling
Why must I continue calling you?

The girl of my dreams
Winnie or Topanga?
Will you leave and remain a friend
Or stay with me forever?

The well-mannered savage
Cotton head, curly-top, nothing like the average
Far from advantageous,
Difficult to manage

Rude boy with nice guy tendencies
Spending every moment striving to be more than a memory
A childhood favorite
Forgotten in your later years
Pouring out my soul
Exposing one of my greatest fears

Meeting the world
One day at a time
In these wonder years
With deep thoughts on the mind

Be still, young heart
Don't run away from the honest
Crushed by the spiteful
No Savage is harmless

Chris A. Lopes
El Cajon, CA

Ben and Fred Savage are somewhat childhood heroes of mine, as uncool as that sounds. Also, I am working on a book inspired by "My Beautiful Dark Twisted Fantasy" by Kanye West. This is the inspiration of "Christian Dior Denim Flow." Lastly, this poem was inspired by love and fear. I really just want to make an impact through art. I want to inspire the obscure and the awkward, the forgotten. I love you all, Rosewood.

251

Don't Put Me Down

Don't put me down because
I don't have the nice things you have!
I may not be rich, but I'm a beautiful person.
I have a perfect smile and perfect attitude.
So, don't put me down because
I'm not the shape you are; small thin, a perfect model.
I'm a healthy, strong woman with four kids whom I love dearly.
I'm a Christian, born and raised in church.
So please, don't put me down!
I believe that I'm putting forth great effort
to become a positive and strong role model.
Just because I'm different and life is not so great,
I have a God who is willing to help me make it through the day.

So please down put me down!

Katrina J. Burrell
Oklahoma, OK

This is my story. My poem is inspired by my family who always said I can do anything I put my mind to. This is for my four angels—Deona, Donna, Adrina, and Shemar—and to my mother Donna M. Fisher.

Hidden Personality

Behind those pretty green eyes,
A sorrowful soul quietly hides
After every heart-breaking fight
She pretends to be alright.
Behind the perky attitude
Is the opposite formation of mood.
Tears are shed as is blood.
Emotions flash like a flood.
She looks in the mirror, not seeing her;
Instead she sees a fake monster.
Her wrists pierce in pain,
What has this to gain?
Acting on impulse is what she's doing.
She's sick and tired of the feuding.
This poor girl has no one to turn to.
It's now time for school, she knows what to do.
She dabs at the blood, throws the towel away,
Puts on a smile to go on for the day.

Cassidy A. Pilling
Denver, CO

I felt this poem covers an aspect of my everyday life. As a teen struggling with depression, it seems that I have two different "personas," one of which is a cover-up to assure others I am okay. Although I have overcome cutting, I still talk about it in most of my poetry. I've recently begun to use poetry as a way to de-stress myself. With two younger sisters (Summer and Jody) following in my footsteps, I have to be a role model and poetry gives me the chance.

Forever

Love you in the morning
When the day is dawning
Love you thru the day
While the sun makes its way
Love you in the twi-light
As the day turns to night
Love you in the moon shine
That makes your beauty fine
Love you even in my sleep
Dreaming dreams so deep
Love you with all my heart
Till from this world I part
Then when we meet once more
We will stroll Heaven's shore
Hand in hand forever
To be without you *never*

Ed Broderick
Rockaway Beach, NY

A Friend's Love

This poem is dedicated to my friend
James Andrew Kelly.

Love is when I see you
And there is sense of joy
You may not always see me
But be assured my friend
Love is always present until the very end

Love is when I hear you
You always make me smile
Your voice is like an angel's song
And this I can't deny

Love is when you comfort me
Sometimes you may not know
Forever bringing calmness
To my tattered soul

Love is when you need me
To listen to you too
Our friendship is enduring
And will last our whole lives through

Wanda L. Haver
Indianapolis, IN

Changes

One day goes by
With never asking why.

Sudden changes in life
Bring us close together
Though tearing us apart
Keeping us close at heart
With never asking why.

September 11 came and went
Now our lives so bent.

Day by day
And
Night by night
New lives are born
Yet still we mourn.

Another day goes by
With now asking why.

We were once strong
Now we are stronger.

One day goes by
With now asking why.

God bless America

Anni G. Schilling
Englewood, CO

I work as a certified pharmacy technician. My father, sister, and eldest brother live here in Colorado. My mom lives in New Hampshire and my other brother lives in California. I was born in the San Francisco Bay area on March 15, 1972. I've struggled with issues in my life; my poems are a way out. All my poetry comes from the heart. What inspired me about writing this poem were the events that took place on September 11, 2001, and all the emotions that stay with us each and every day.

Your Shoes

I've been where you are
I've gotten that news
I know what it's like to be in your shoes
But don't give up, have faith and hope
And believe in the good Lord to bring you through
I'm not going to lie; it won't be an easy ride
But the faith and hope will bring you through the scary times
And when you want help call on Him
For He will listen to all that is being said
His ears are open at any time
And He will guide you through your weakest times
He will hold you and love you for you are his child
And when the pain is rough give the world your biggest smile
I know it's not easy to face the world
With a bald head and dark circles under your eyes
But remember you're never alone
I know you want to be angry at times
But remember this
Anger doesn't deserve the time
I've been where you are
I've gotten that news
I know what it's like to be in your shoes

Sarah R. Boyter
Advance, NC

Behind the Shadows

What is it to be different?
How hard do we try to be the same?
What is it like to just be me all of the time?
At home in my room I am an individual I am different,
But when people are near, when I'm in the halls at school, and in the
classrooms I am no longer me, I am no longer different.
People look at me and see right through me, they do not notice the
trail of a tear on my cheek, or the loneliness surrounding me, or the
     talent that I posses.
I disappear in the crowd with my normal looking clothes and no sign
     of a smile.
In school I am expected to only laugh when I am supposed to,
talk when I am supposed to talk, and not to be noticed too much.
That is what other people think normal is and should always be.
I have to make myself seem normal so that they do not see me as
     different, so that they will accept me.
I am terrified of people's judgment even though I pretend that I'm
not and that I do not care what other people think of me.
I am different when I am alone I am me, I look different when
nobody is around to watch me with disapproving eyes, and I do what
I love to do when there is nobody there trying to change me and
     criticize me.
I know who I am but I am not brave enough or ready to let everyone
else know who I am because the judgment and punishment is just too
     much.

Katie Larsen
West Jordan, UT

The Ocean's Gem

Thick, yet pure, sheets of blue,
Curved tips frayed white.
Years of experience, guarding life.
Barely known life held by fragile hands,
Free, yet bound to Earth by heavy bands.
Thick, then flows thin.
Can rip away so much,
Yet once contained can be untouched.
Eyes searching back and forth
For something much more valued than it's worth.
Wait, what's that?
Something Mother Nature's kept under lock and key,
Certainly it is worthy of me!
Push it close, listen up!
What do you hear?
I hear thunder!
Well, that's your plunder!
I hear a crash, a sound of power,
Yet as delicate as a flower.
It slices through whatever,
Yet leaving it unharmed.
But know this now, Mother Nature comes armed.

Madelyn C. Hansen
Richmond Hill, GA

Bio

I'm deranged, my soul needs to be rearranged, my life I'd love to
    exchange
I'm a paradox, so f***ing unorthodox
I am the Grim Reaper, an organ soul keeper
Fallen from grace, falling from space, I'm such a disgrace
Narcissistic and so sadistic
A sweet switchblade knife and a tongue like a razor, loving to hate
    all the haters
I'm so perfect and so dead that I'm beautiful, with nothing left that's
    meaningful
Misanthropy will always be inside of me
I'm just a pointless mosquito, of my libido
I'm a violent, sex-filled, drugged face—armored tank, but still such
    an empty filled plate
Eating away at every single part of me I'm stolen, with a heart that's
    swollen
I am an atrophy because something's inside of me
I'm just a little f***ing boy because I have no spleen, do you really
    wanna take a bite out of my mystery machine?

James P. Licari
Patchogue, NY

What inspired me to write this poem was in general, life. The pros and cons of life,
how to cope and deal with them and how to get through it. Life can also be misery if
you want it to be. This poem was about me debasing myself because I want people
to realize that you are no better than I am, and I am no better than you are. I wanted
people to stop being blinded, open up their eyes and see things for what they really are.

Melancholy

Wrapped in sadness, I let my soul
drift in a roiling sea,
overcome by the storm that engulfs me.

Waves wash over and around me.
In the dark, I am tossed
on a cold ocean of doubts; I am lost.

No signal flare to call for help,
no proffered hand of hope
to calm the journey, no anchoring rope.

Now and again I dive into
my swirling sea of doubt
and embrace the sadness with silent shout,

and swim alone in my own thoughts—
I wonder what might be
as darkened waters cleanse and set me free.

Kim H. Sherman
Eugene, OR

Carried Away

He was her prince in shining armor, but to him he was your average guy,
yet this was someone she had always dreamed about as a little girl.
To her, he was everything she could ever ask for and perfect in every way.
She will only once be given this, to either look away or to plunge in
with every emotion that becomes her, and somehow their worlds will
collide. Yet she will not look back, only then they can be together.
He welcomed her with open arms and made her feel secure. His body
seems to overpower hers and yet she is not afraid. He gives her hope
to go on and makes her feel safe. His words are spoken to her so eloquently,
and he has been places she has never seen. He carries an energy for
them, so that she can set herself free. They laugh, they love and their
bond will be something people only search for and yet never find.
He completely is consumed by her and she is lucky to have known him.
She remembers his smile and his lips are dry and cracked of neglect
and yet it's imprinted in her mind. She is totally captivated by his hands
and his fingers are long and sleek as she rubs them between hers.
Softly their fingers meet and she will be taken in by that very moment.
She takes her hand and touches his strong arms as it shows all his strength,
and yet they know one day their love will lead them back to a place
they call their own.

Linda J. Atteo
Mount Prospect, IL

Linda Atteo grew up in a middle class, Catholic upbringing, and having three sisters,
trying to get attention or a word in edgewise at the dinner table was easier said than
done. At a young age, Linda found herself writing in order to bring some solace
into her life and so she turned to poetry as a way of expressing her thoughts and
emotions which she found too difficult to express with her family and friends. It was
her own way of releasing her feelings; when things were difficult, she always knew
that writing would give her peace. Then a time came in her life where she felt alone
and became withdrawn. The inspiration for this poem is about someone very special
who brought her happiness and encouraged her to believe in herself. This poem is
a tribute to all who have fallen hard. Know there is someone waiting for you, who
will love you for you. Believe in yourself and know you will be okay.

Loving a Dying Child

To live is an illusion,
To die is reality.
A baby is born to them,
The child gazes at his world.
Those they love live in that son,
and his eyes show wonder, awe.
If time was never-ending,
Perhaps his heart could live on.
For their blood is with that child,
The desire to live shines.
Life is not forever though,
Death will strike the ones they love.
Disease is a mere engine,
Death is its pulpit that shines.
A child with deadly murmurs,
His heart is dying slowly.
A child to die with love,
With the care that he deserves.
The glimpse of hope these parents
share is nothing more than done.
All that they knew to be true
will vanish from their own eyes.
They enjoy moments they have,
For living will not last long.
To die is reality,
To live is an illusion.

Aditya Rengaswamy
Troy, MI

Going Green

Going green is not hard;
It can start in your own back yard.

Plant a tree, and watch it grow;
See how far your green can go!

Ride together on your way to school,
You and your friend could carpool.

This can help save gasoline,
It is all part of going green.

Incandescent, halogen, and LED, too.
Try using a compact fluorescent to help you.

Every twirl-y light bulb saves
Energy we can use each day.

Reduce, reuse, recycle is the next part.
Going green will make us smart.

We can be a green nation;
Starting with preservation.

There are items we can use
Over and over, it is your turn to choose.

It's all about going green;
A better way for you and me!

Courtney L. Zych
Gretna, NE

Two Strangers, Two Friends

Perchance to see the naked sky,
with a glimmering moon on a glimmering night.
Long, deep breath with an exhaled sigh,
no more reason, no more try.

Perchance to see the bright shine,
in a forged temple, in a forged shrine.
Nevertheless to make you mine,
no more reason, no more try.

Perchance to see our first dance,
with our love, with life's chance.
So beautiful I have seen in a glance, yet,
no more reason, no more try.

Perchance to hold a hand,
helpless boyhood, helpless man.
Wishing to forever wear love's band, still,
no more reason, no more try.

Perchance to wait 'til death,
nevertheless, never the rest,
of waiting beyond my selfless best,
giving me reason, and making me try.

Samuel R. Rose
Columbus, WI

This Mystery of Me

I am who I am,
that is all I will ever be.
I reveal very little,
and I leave the rest
a mystery.

You don't know my next move,
or what I'm going to do.
I'm not going to tell you,
I'd like to keep you guessing
as I bid you all,
oh sweet adieu....

I don't know how I'm going to hide it
and keep you all from knowing
This Mystery of Me
that you can't figure out.

And this information I'm not showing,
time will tell if I reveal This Mystery
and let you all see;
time will tell if I reveal This Mystery…

This Mystery of Me….

Richard E. Remick
Plainview, NY

The Journey

The path strays
my hope is tight
I pray to Heaven
the choice is right.
I walk steadily
my fear explodes
With shivers and shakes
hearing who knows.
The wind attacks
my scarf unrolls
Scrambling the ground
missing my toes.
Pushing forward
stomping away
The wind whispers
leading the way.
My hands so cold
the feeling of ice
Numbs my body
and paying the price.
The trip hence done
my hope at still
Night then falls
taking my will.

Heather A. Searfoss
Mechanicsburg, PA

Choice

Young mother, he slid behind your turned back;
Watching and waiting, you wonder which tack
His conscience will take.... O Happy Day
When shame wins out, and you pardon his way.

Though love forgives, yet consequence is clear;
And you help your son pay the cost so dear
By holding his hand and leading the way
Through whatever penalty he must pay.

Wise woman! And did you always know
The path this trial was bound to go?
Or did you learn through error and loss
The way to lead a child to the cross?

He might not stay there, but you understand,
That choice is given to every young man;
Many are old ere they finally know
That Heaven is a place they want to go.

God is Father, and family is knit,
If God is not loved then a man won't fit;
And although you yearn to carry him through,
That choice is his, just as yours was for you.

Alice R. Shoaf
Maricopa, AZ

I Am with You and You Are with Me

Daddy,
when I giggle, I hear you laughing
When I weep, I hear you crying
When I sleep, I hear you snoring
When I get out of bed in the morning,
I look for you as I look up to the sky
I know you're looking down at me
But I can't see you? Why can't I?
I close my eyes and you rescue me
like I'm a princess in our bedtime fables.
Drifting on pearl cotton candy clouds with beautiful angels
Flying faster than the birds and bees
We are the wind through the trees
Flying higher above the shimmering turquoise sea
I am with you and you're with me
We glide our fingertips through the fairy dust stars
Through the amethyst sky to the moon and up to Mars
When I open my eyes I will be back in my bed
With a smile on my face because I know you're not dead
Gazing up to the sky I can see you this time
You're the man in the moon, the breeze in the afternoon
The light in the stars,
soaring through Mars.
You're the wind in the trees,
the birds and the bees
I am with you and you are with me.

Jenna B. Goldman
Beverly Hills, CA

I was inspired to write this poem about death, when my father unexpectedly passed away last year. I am twenty-one years old, and I have two brothers. I have always been a daddy's girl and his only girl. I wrote this poem from the little girl inside me, in which I found strength and the power to heal. When someone dies, they are still with you and you are still with them. My father's spirit is all around me and he will forever live in me.

Special Moments

A beautiful face in a white dress glides down an aisle meant for her.
A handsome face anticipates her arrival at the other side.
Dragonflies visit from the nearby pond and buzz through the crowd,
Lingering near the strongest stenches of perfume.
Faces with smiles, faces with tears,
All gather in the silence for the special moment.
The special moment when the most important words ring clear:
I do.

Morgan M. Miller
Montgomery, IL

Rose of Fate

A beautiful rose grows peacefully.
It lives its life to the fullest
Making everyone around it feel loved and cared for.
Shining in the moonlight,
Blooming reds and growing ever so peacefully.
See its end.
Watch it slowly fade away.
Its petals floating in the wind,
Flying through the angel lit sky
Going through Heaven's gates then back to where it has died,
as people wipe tears away from their eyes.
They don't have to cry anymore; God's angel is here.
Look to the heavens and praise His holy name.
Another rose will take its place and show the same love and faith …

Zakiya C. Williams
Riverdale, GA

Deep Sleeper

The hushed murmur rises to a deafening whisper.
I lounge wistfully, with feet up and head back,
In the tiny room sandwiched between dream and present.
My eyelids do not flutter. My head does not twitch.
The employ of my title startles
And goads me through the door to now.
Not my name. My title.
The deafening whisper rises to a pitch of clarity.
"Awake, O' Sleeper."
The "S" strikes my gut, stealing the air from my lungs.
I'm reminded of a child, an oak, a branch, a fall, the ground.
My eyelids now ajar, my head now stirring.
My eyes wade through the heavy darkness to find the author of,
The murmur, the whisper, and the pitch.
I'm still. Very still.
The pitch of clarity rises to a muffled yell.
"Awake, O' Sleeper!"
My heart generates the sound of a stallion sprinting.
I'm convinced the whole world can hear it,
And cringe apologetically.
I flip a switch; the light wraps my room in a warm, searing embrace.
But I sit there frozen. Icy silence.
"How do you know me?"
The question weakly slips out of my mouth,
Like a worm nearing death.
The muffled yell rises to a thunderous cry.
"Awake, O' Sleeper!" Fear taps out.
Anger steps in the ring to face the unrelenting indictment.
I stand upon my bed and bellow at
The ceiling, the roof, the sky, the universe.
"But the days are evil! The days are evil!"
I catch my breath and there is only quiet.

Joel T. Sappington
Glendale, CA

Remember Me

Remember me when I am gone;
    Gone far away into another land.
Remember me when the sun no longer shines on me,
    When I'm buried beneath the sand.

Remember all the good times;
    Even remembering the sad.
Remember the bonds that tie us together;
    For the good times and the bad.

Remember me when you are feeling low,
    For I will be there to comfort.
Remember that even in my absence,
    You will never be alone.

Remember me when you feel lost,
    and there's no one to light your way.
Remember me and keep your faith,
    I will be there to guide you, to show you the way.

Remember me when you feel alone,
    with no one left to trust.
Remember my warm embrace,
    remember my soft words and loving touch.

Remember me always my friend,
    As I will be watching over you forever.
Here I will be waiting for you, my dear friend,
    until the day we meet again.

Jamie P. Merrill
Phoenix, AZ

Dreamer

I have always been a dreamer,
But it often causes pain.
It has even left me standing, crying in the rain.
If dreams could change tomorrow, would it all be the same?
Or would it be forgotten, like a story without fame?
Sometimes life is uncertain, without anyone to blame.
Like a starving wild animal, not even God himself can tame.
I have always been a dreamer, I walk a higher plane.
But it often leaves me feeling lost and insane,
Kind of like a picture that never fit a frame.
Would I be remembered if I did not have a name?
It is really hard to focus without all the rules to the game.
No way to get off of this out of control train.
Are there really dreams that don't cause strain?
What is it all about, what have I become?

Altina L. Yonker
Gervais, OR

Summer

In the summertime flowers start to bloom.
The smell of the flowers smell like nice perfume.
If you are sweating and want to get cool,
You can go swimming in the pool.
Summer is that time of year when you have no school.
You can hang out with your friends
Or go to a party over the weekend.
You could always take a vacation
Or just stay home.
In summer you can just relax
And you don't have to carry around a heavy backpack.
But summer doesn't last forever.
But sooner or later, summer will be coming back around the corner.

Hannah R. Glasser
Pittsburgh, PA

No Precedence

I call out to my love seeking a warm, welcoming embrace,
Eerily, my echo returns to me as shadows hide his face.
Suddenly, every breath feels weighted, like chains wrapped around
    my chest,
Now, sinking into dark abyss, to survive I try my best.
Each pain-staking second becomes more elongated than the last,
Drifting into the Netherlands I try to reconcile with my past.
Novelty endings hold no precedence in this tragic, modern, fairy tale,
For my soul aimlessly drifts along forever condemned to emotional jail.

Erica Ella Craig
Sussex, NJ

Missing Pieces

Sometimes I sit in my room and think about you.
I know you're gone, but I still feel you.
When I'm having a bad day,
You somehow still comfort me.
When I need someone there for me,
It's like you never left.
Some days I think of where we'd be now.
And some I think about never saying goodbye.
Knowing you're gone forever kills me inside.
I want one last hug from you.
I want you to read me a bedtime story.
I feel you beside me before I fall asleep.
My heart feels like it's missing a piece
My heart hurts when I see your name
Or even pictures of you.
I'm missing a piece of me.
I'm missing you.

Jakaya M. Quire
South Wayne, WI

Beethoven's Golden Note

I hear the music in my sleep.
Wisps of notes I choose to keep.
Around me nights and days on end,
And in my head they twist and bend.
A noisy flow of continuous joy,
And not a beat would I destroy.
Careful, sweet and delicate sounds,
Or striking rhythms come in rounds.
Like a music box that plays all day,
That music, it never goes away.
It comes in colors orange and red.
I long to say what's in my head.
In my heart a kindling fire.
To let it out is my desire.
Swirling around against my brain,
And coming down like a gentle rain.
I hear this symphony not through my ears.
Frustration comes in soggy tears.
My heart hears what my pen can't write.
Too high to reach with all my might.
Yet the notes drone on and on inside,
Like the rise and fall of a weary tide.
A crescendo of a musical cry,
A fermata from which I cannot hide.
Though these sounds I can't escape,
Music is the noblest fate.
A never-ending golden note,
One that God himself hath wrote.

Hannah E. Bauer
Granville, OH

Would You?

If I was a Marine,
and I went away,
would you miss me?

If I found a gem
worth a million dollars,
would you dance?

If I was being picked on by bullies,
and my feelings were hurt,
would you stand up for me?

If I was bankrupt
and needed a home,
would you let me in?

If I was in an accident,
and was in the hospital,
would you visit me?

If my mother died,
and I was in pieces,
would you comfort me?

If I said I loved you,
and secretly,
you loved me too,
would you tell me?

If I knelt on the ground
and asked you to marry me,
would you say yes?

Antonia Uchytil
Holly Ridge, NC

Be Free

Be free little girl
  from father's words
    spoken and unspoken

From uncaring look
  and move and silence,
    shouting uncertainty
    and fear

Planted in a child's mind
  to bloom in times
    like now.

Be free young girl
  from judgement heard
    as from God Himself

But coming only
  from a man
    who broken too

Hears what is said
  from parent past
    as if from God

Be free young woman
  from prison place
    of doubt
      and "wonder if"
      and "worst case" tho'ts

From that which
  binds and stifles
    breath and life

And blinds the sight
  from seeing
    and believing
      what could really be . . .
      If free.

Gary L. Evans
Mesilla, NM

When I, I Find

When I seek his face,
I find his grace.

When I am still,
I find his will.

When I look above,
I find his love.

When I give him my cares,
I find him there.

When I seek his story,
I find his glory.

When I kneel and pray,
I find him in my day.

When I don't know where to go,
I find he restores my soul.

When I feel I just can't stand,
I find his nail-pierced hand.

When I feel life is just too much,
I find his gentle touch.

When I feel close to tears,
I find his words, "Have no fear."

When I see life going according to plan,
I find it's my faith in the great "I AM."

Linda K. Taskey
Spokane, WA

I am a single mother of two sons and one daughter, and grandmother of two grandsons and four granddaughters. My poetry has always been inspired by my great love for Jesus Christ, my Lord and Saviour. I truly believe God's Holy Spirit inspires me to write and pass my poetry along to family and friends, for his purpose. I give God the glory for all my poetry. They are truly a gift from God.

Frozen Dreams

I left the valley some time ago
To find solitude and peace of mind
Now I'm high on a mountain far from home
Living in a cabin just killing time

The sound of nature is my only company
And a burning candle to lighten the night
No radio or cable TV
Just a memory of the love of my life

I hear a moan whisper in the wind
It sounds like my own heart's cry
How I miss my one and only friend
Who no longer can be by my side

I watch each season come to a change
And how slowly they pass me by
When alone in a wilderness that has no name
Only God may know if I'm still alive

I can feel a cold chill in the air
Soon it will whiten the forest and streams
Leaving foot steps of a man without a care
Facing another winter of only frozen dreams.

Wayne E. Christie
Clackmas, OR

If I Were the Mayor of Daddytown

If I were the mayor of Daddytown,
I'd climb in Dad's lap and sit right down.
I would laugh and laugh like a silly clown
If I were the mayor of Daddytown!

If I were the mayor of Daddytown.
My daddy would wear a golden crown
Instead of a wrinkled hat of brown,
If I were the mayor of Daddytown!

If I were the mayor of Daddytown,
My dad would always be around.
I'd make it illegal for dads to frown
If I were the mayor of Daddytown!

If I were the mayor of Daddytown,
There would be no drug abuse in my town."
So my dad's mind would always be sound
If I were the mayor of Daddytown!

If I were the mayor of Daddytown,
I'd say, "I love you, Dad, please put that down."
And maybe my dad would still be around
If I were the mayor of Daddytown!

Modestine W. Brody
Florence, SC

The Donkey That Glowed

Sometimes there is gold
but are you willing to sell?
Her soul will go alone
forever tormented by a spell.

Bitter but sweet
Elane was the name
incoherent of oneself
a puppet she laid.

No one to call friend
wished so badly to be changed
the star didn't twinkle every night
she was at end.

Sometimes there is gold
but are you willing to sell?
Her soul will go alone
forever tormented by a spell.

One evening, she went to the mysterious man and said
She had two nickels and a toad
"I want to glow as if I were a moon"
"I beg you, so I could be worthy of, not a dead crow."

The mysterious man gave her one choice
"Give me your soul and I'll give you gold."
When she took the gold, she glowed alright
A fool she looked and an ass with no soul.

Alyssa A. Howes-Corriea
Shelby, NC

words

the moment has passed
that instant when
your words hang
in the air
just before impact
that last second
when you can call them back
when you still own them
the moment has passed
and the words
that tumbled from my lips
have touched you
and are gone
forever

Karen A. Hofmann
Mt. Laurel, NJ

The Commander

Hut! Two! I march like a soldier.
One! Two! I turn at a signal.
Company, march! I say, "Yes, sir!"
I spot a boat at the border.

The boat is the enemy's.
It is in my line of fire,
And I fire my RPG.
The boat is destroyed. Oh yes, sir!

Overnight I am a hero.
I received honors and medals.
I am promoted. Bingo!
I am among the generals.

Alexandre E. Samy
San Diego, CA

Through the Forest

As I'm walking,
I am talking
Through the forest trees.
Kicking rocks,
Watching a fox
Enjoying the nice, cool breeze.

Bundling up in my warm coat.
Watching the clouds as they float.
Stepping in the cold, white snow.
Having fun
Since this day has begun.
But soon it'll be time to go.

I'll get in bed,
And cover up my head,
Until I fall asleep.
I won't come out,
And start wandering about,
Until' I'm done counting sheep!

Mya J. Dupree
Mesa, AZ

Heartless

I take my last breath in, which ends in a gasp of pain,
really, will I ever be free from sorrow's reigns?

I look at the sky now pouring down dust and debris,
and I start to wonder where this life leaves me.

My future was never clear and I thought I'd found the one, but it's
time dear,
to stop lying to me with each breath you take,

Because now I finally gathered up the strength to look the beast in
you in the eye,
and it's you he despised all these years.

I wish that for just one moment in time you could feel this,
and know what Hell truly is,

Especially the one you have created for me to live my life in,
but you'd never feel the pain nor the anger.

I believe that your heart went cold a long time ago,
numbing your body and soul to any feeling or emotion.

You are truly void of everything.

Maybe perhaps it is because you created a void within you,
to keep your heart, soul, and body impenetrable to us.

Shiloh M. Abrams
Argillite, KY

I've been writing poetry since I was fifteen years old. Since then it's been a great
passion of mine. When I write, everything comes to me from a thought or feeling.
I wrote this poem when I was in a very deep and nostalgic mood. I decided to sit
down and write about it in a way that expressed my exact mood and thoughts at the
time. This piece has a great amount of emotion in it like sorrow and pain. It even
has the feeling of being triumphant about being able to overcome someone who held
a negative hold on you.

French Orleans

The streets like lungs full of the hazy air.
The swanky sultry sweat of the city rising and settling in my bones.
Everything breathes.
Everything sings its own song, full of the bluesy swells and throaty moans.
The air is dense with passion, the walls transpire with soul.
Heat—it is all around me: up, down, left, right and inside me.
Time is held prisoner to the night, for it ceases to subsist on the
    streets of the Big Easy.
Laughs and music pound their way into my consciousness, stirring
    my own song within me.
My heart synchronizes with its melody, beating the slow drum.
My fingertips feel the sway and swoon of the sound.
The saxophone, sweet and sincere, singing in my blood.
The heart of this City pulsates within me.
I am its lover.
I leave my Sagacity in bed to sleep, while I consume in my transient
    harmony with the City.
The fire within me settles, and I satisfy that latent animal side within.
My Indulgence is my treasured secret.
And although distant, the Lost City remains forever found within me.

Priscilla Rosario
North Bergen, NJ

all the little pieces

all the little pieces
scattered on the floor;
happy, little memories
like shells upon the shore.

fragile little moments
brought in by your tides;
short bittersweet seconds
taken all in strides.

tiny little pieces,
fragments of my heart,
without you in my life
quickly fall apart.

pieced together beautiful;
undone, a shattered mess.
you are the keystone,
without your love regress.

without the mold love provides
in waves, the pieces wade,
waiting upon your return
but too other beaches fade.

so return, love, to the coast,
once more so I can say,
the mosaic is incomplete
without you in every day.

all the little pieces
will together renew,
when you come home again
and echo my love for you.

Kevin J. Mauter
Orlando, FL

Never Again

Never again
will I feel my heart flutter
or bleed out of love
although I'm a cutter

Never again
will I breathe without air
or open my heart
for someone to share

Never again
can I feel my heart race
or have someone's arms
be my happy place

Never again
will I have what I feel
or stop my dreaming
'cause I love what is real

Never again
can I have a happy end
Will I ever fall in love?
No, never again

Evalie V. Graham
Ft. Lauderdale, FL

The Soldier in a Foreign Land

Edwin Aulding, rich as any,
gilded armor and wealth a plenty,
raised his head as he walked through town,
thinking he wore the Emperor's new gown.

But no one could see the battle raging inside,
between Edwin's sick heart and his gentleman's mind.
With feet on cobblestone he turned to see
the simple man's boy whom he longed to be.

The sickness inside begged and silently pleaded
for its twisted ideas to be universally heeded.
But his mind knew better, people fixed his brain,
so it subdued at once these longings insane.

Edwin could not say or write what he wanted,
but simple boy could act out his wishes undaunted.
Pampered Edwin was not to play in the fields,
a man of his type must be training with shields.

And as Edwin rounded the corner, sword in hand,
the peasants glared at him, conqueror of their land.
He tried to destroy the only question in his heart,
which was "Maybe we're all equal, and not so apart."

Farhan Kathawala
Memphis, TN

Life's Plunder

I look into the sky
when I'm alone in the night
although the moon's not bright
As I search across the night
hoping, dreaming for the light
it's too much to live in bliss
it's too little to live in fright
its to hard to try and fight
I'm in a desert but have lost my site
for me without you
is the sun without moon
and I know that soon
when I look at a heart left in ruin
then I know it is you
I won't know what to do
when I look upon you I wish only happiness
I want you to know you are missed
by a soul left to wander
I am one with my plunder
and when life is the thunder
you are the rain
and life without you
is a life of pain

Asa P. Hutchins
Caucasian, IL

Suicidal Idiocies for Life's Deficiencies

Suicide has such an overwhelmingly sadistic,
succumbing seduction when pain seems so severely inevitable
to treat or avoid its grip based on our abilities, or lack thereof,
to not only recognize much more appealing emotions linked to suicide,
but also to discipline the monitoring of our personal thoughts and actions
into the seemingly impossible thoughts surrounding the actions
of inspirational survival as well as the persevering passion
for the ultimate recovery from such severely damaging excuses
suicide attempts to create as a self-fulfilling validation
for what a pathetic, worthless ambition it has been for you to have lived,
to keep living, and to have ambition's true, authentic glory fulfilled
only through the joyful, exuberant eternity given to us after death
life could only dream about waking up to its never ceasing reality
we can't even imagine its existence of until we are dead.
In this contradicting sense of our battle between the reality realized
every day we continue to live versus the extremely cumbersome,
intensely overbearing obscurity of a death that has never realized
its depth of reality until it has been finalized in only one day's actions,
it seems like a more profitable ambition to force death's one opportunity
for the ultimate glory of your life to take a much more natural,
healthier course of action that only life has numerous opportunities
for not only securing the glory strengthened by living a life free from
    obscurity,
but also securing the glory strengthened by a much more subdued,
    peaceful death
leading to a much stronger sense of exuberant eternity
suicide only seeks to destroy and severely downplay the significant
worth of your life before and throughout all of your existing eternity.
Live a great life rather than dying every day you could have been alive
waiting for death's eventual obscurity validated through your willingness
in living a highly fulfilling, significant life others will envy to imitate
your life giving example in rejecting Suicidal Idiocies for Life's
    Deficiencies
by indulging in Life's Unbelievably Potential Sufficiencies.

William M. Darrah
Amarillo, TX

This poem is dedicated to Troy Salmon. He was a great friend that I grew up with. He committed suicide in 2004 at the age of twenty-four. I was adopted at the age of four by two amazing, patient, incredibly loving parents who always made my education their biggest priority. Ironically, I despised writing in high school until I met Bruce McGinnis, my Amarillo College professor. He is now retired. His abundantly creative love for poetry deeply mesmerized me forever. My poetry became much more personalized when I dated Tiffany Bryant, my first true love in 2000. Thanks, Mom and Dad, for always encouraging my shy personality so I could enjoy writing.

The Next Step

Insight 1:
There are two types of persons in the world:
those who want assistance ascending stairs
and those who wish to rise unaided.

Personal Reflection 1:
With this whiskey degrading my dendrites
and my lucidity on the verge of extinction,
I feel surprisingly sober and frightfully complete.
But will someone please direct my next step?

Insight 2:
In the vacuum of ordinary life,
solace may be found in exerting conviction
beyond the near escape.

Personal Reflection 2:
I have seen, many times, the trickling waterfall,
the one that variably dries, day-by-day,
and I must say that I have seen worse testaments to life.

Insight 3:
There is an incurable plague that has spread rampantly for centuries,
and when man merges with machine and technology transcends biology,
and though new cures and remedies shall be provided with the
coming ages
none yet will be potent enough to purge the world of this
aforementioned plague.
For even to speak its name spreads it disease: Boredom.

Personal Reflection 3:
No matter what I do, who I am with, what I learn, read and write,
it will always become tedious to me, and will always, eventually,
bore me. Am I boring?

Brian Martin
Hinsdale, NH

The inspiration for all artists, however prolific or unknown, has no enigmatic origin;
it is born form the direct experiences with even the most mundane of circumstances.
It often resides obscured in the peripheral, begging us to take notice of a seemingly
insignificant detail. There is no end to inspiration; there is only one's resolve to
seek it. For myself and the poems I write all the subject matter derives from family,
friends, books, the infinitude of modern media, and nature. I owe thanks to all those
who have been close to me who have helped me prosper.

My Song to Sing

I could count my money
but I'd rather count my blessings
I'd rather get lost in song
and find myself progressing
with an open mind
Ideas shared
learning through life's lessons
listening to music, reading books
writing poetry, finding that connection
In this world of heartache and tragedy
one must truly believe
listen intensely to your soul
find your song to sing
Music is a powerful, moving
ever-evolving thing
healing and connecting us
through: verse, hymn, phrase—we sing
When the heavens above are all lit up
hear the angels sing
We are connected to them
in all that music brings
A life enriched through music
somehow in passing shall sing
into a world of wonder
A soul that now has wings.

Kelli Kay Day
Hurricane, WV

Me and You Forever, Love

First born among three.
Thirst for life never fed.
Burst, is the verb of my heart.
Me! First to leave my bed.

Right away I was led astray.
Light could not pierce the dark days.
Fight is what I told myself.
And right then I found God's ways.

Strong will, strong mind, strong hands.
Wrong ways inflicted by pain.
Long were the days I played unfaithful.
You! Strong boy I met in the rain.

Is this love really real?
This thing that started from nothing new.
Bliss is still what you gave me.
Forever is what I want with you.

Save me from debauchery.
Pave the way for better days.
Grave is the face of the parents that birthed me.
Love, save me from these ways.

I'll say this once more love, me and you forever?

Gabrielle A. Wong
Miramar, FL

Thank You

I've never had a Valentine
or belonged before this day
It is this year you came along
that's brought me now to say

I'm sorry for my crying
my tears and all my faults
Thank you for understanding
that life is not a waltz

You got me through my trials
when I doubted I'd survive
You taught me how to navigate
through life, so I would strive
To find out life's true meaning
to know there's something there
that makes each life worth living
and that we make quite a pair

Lori C. Scott
Augusta, GA

Devil in Disguise

So you sold your soul to the Devil. When will you ever learn?
First, she destroys your will, leaving only embers to burn.
There's just no stopping her. Once she's put out the flame.
She loves to see you suffer. It's just part of her game.

Have you forgotten all the things that's she's done?
Treating you rotten, just for fun?
You've been here before, you should know what to do.
Head for the door if you know what's good for you!

Don't look back. There's nothing there.
But a world that lacks, someone you thought cared.
So open your eyes! She's the Devil, you see…
the "Devil in Disguise" who will never let you be free.

Carol A. Sarner
Saugus, CA

Moments

The days go by
We live, we work
We do all the things that make our lives, our lives
Some days seem strange
Detached, like a missing page
Still there, though
It's like you can step back and see
But you don't understand
It's just another day
All the things are happening that make it another day
Yet at any moment it can change though
Things happen, as they say
All we have is this moment
When the moment passes it's gone forever
What do we do with these moments?
What do we do with our time?

All the philosophy in the world cannot save us from time
It runs on
In spite of us it keeps going
You feel like you're not moving forward
Stagnant, stuck
Losing moments and gaining nothing
All we have is this moment
Then the moment's gone
What do the moments of our lives equal?
What have we become?

Chris Bush
Mishawaka, IN

winter rhododendron

once waxy green leaves that spiraled
wide droop now mourning a sun
that has not shown its face
this december day
leaves now almost black
against snow-covered ground
drop downward like half closed
umbrellas as if gaining warmth
from their closeness
I will watch patiently
for spring warmth
to stir their life juices
when winter dark leaves
open themselves once again
to the warm sun

Lois Howarth-Davis
Akron, OH

My Fake Reality

What has the world come to these days?
Reality is just so fake. The TV shows…all scripted.
People these days think they are so perfect.
Does that mean my life is fake and pretend too? Is my life made up
    of lies?
"She doesn't know it, but when people tell her she's beautiful
They're telling her the truth. So she may be a little klutzy, but who cares?
That just makes her who she is."
Why do people lie to me?
I look in the mirror and what do I see? I see not what others seem to see
I see an ugly duckling.
"As we see a swan who's gorgeous as can be, not knowing her true beauty
and what lies beneath."
So I may be a little blonde, some people don't like it;
but yet they tell me that they love my personality.
They make fun of me and laugh at me all the time.
"We laugh and make fun because we love. We love when you fall up stairs
or make up words no one knows. We love your personality. Who doesn't?"
My life seems so fake. Reality is not real.
"But your life is real. S*** happens, dreams can come true."
I want to run and hide.
"But don't run and hide because your fake reality is nothing but a
    misunderstanding. Everything in your life has and will be real.
So reality shows are scripted; your life isn't.
So people try to act perfect; you know no one is."
One day, just one day
I hope to wake up and everything just isn't fake anymore.
I wish that one day my fake reality just wasn't fake.

Jamie Wine
Rolling Meadow, IL

My Little Sister Jacey

"Don't leave me, let me come too..."
My fragile sister with eyes of blue,
innocently smiling in a jumper of pink
with a purple grey poodle, one wouldn't think
that this girl sucking her finger—she knew...

Frazzled hair and a soft, "Play with me."
Putting on my shoes—oh how I couldn't see
the effects of a distraught family torn
by death, as green as the stains on my knee.
Our mother—so frayed and worn...

Sticky jammy fingers add; "Kira, Mommy is..."
But stop mid-sentence and thought with a kiss
upon my embarrassingly short hair
caused by a mother with no more capability to care.
A funny look, quick to pass, Jacey's distress...

"Play with Connor, okay?" I reply.
Time for my school, she looks about to cry.
Big brother Taylor can't find his shoes.
She'll be okay, I return to my constructed lie
made to save me from reality's blues...

Brown hair bobs, Jacey nods
wise beyond her years, holding back the sobs.
"I love you, okay?"
The deception crumbles, it is not okay.
Imagination—pulling me quickly back—follows its jobs...

"I love you too."
Leaving Jacey on the stoop
I follow my brother. Misery's rule
is to love company, and despair quietly does
follow me as I say, "See you after school."

Kira D. Ashley
Medford, OR

The Hunt for a Passionate Beginning

The hunt for a passionate beginning, the eventual conquest in life,
Once grasped, may bring anew that which I wish I knew.
A chance for mindful circumstance, a release of inner elegance;
Wandering in the fallow artist's shoes.

The prized grain amidst the beaches of life, the mysterious echo to be,
In time, will be told in no manner late nor old.
In season of rightful reason, in perception unlikely beaten;
There escapes the inception of the bold.

This is the time in which I know of living in that fallow artist's shoes,
This is the time in which I've longed to experience simple life anew.

Cooper D. Foster
Lunenburg, MA

Darkness

Glazed wanton night breathes delicate azure hues growing
fields of golden thoughts.

Black stars fall from grace.
Mid-night moons, filled green, greys of gold.

souls slip quick...

Holy wars bleed underground hatred
as old as time—
Bridges burn bright infinite hate.....

Jennifer L. Aldrich
Celoron, NY

Dear Matthew

I wanted to write you a poem,
But then I wanted to write you a letter.
I didn't know which would be better.
Then I thought I could do both.
Here are some things I want you to know.
I wanted to wait for you because I thought you would want me again.
Then we could become more than just friends
But now I'm figuring out every time you walk away
You won't want me tomorrow, you don't want me today.
Waiting for you caused so much pain.
I didn't want to play the game.
But you were the prize, so I pushed through.
That's how much I wanted you.
I'm figuring out even if I won, you wouldn't even care.
I have to say, that's not very fair.
So I'm doing what's best for me and I'm saying goodbye.
I don't want to keep living a lie.
I've given my best endeavor,
But it didn't work, so goodbye forever.

Marisa Wagner
Hutto, TX

This poem was inspired by a boy. I fell in love with him and I thought he felt the same way. Well, he didn't and my heart broke. I tried so hard to get him back, but it didn't work. I was so upset. He was my everything. I then realized that being sad wasn't getting me anywhere. I got up and decided to work my way over him. I wrote him one last goodbye poem, and this is the poem I wrote! I have to say, even though he hurt me, I sure got a good poem out of it!

Dreams of Winter

Cold the wind blows
over the freshly fallen snow,
stirring dreams of winter.

Crystalline ferns grow on windowpane
ice skating on the pond down the lane,
house eve and tree limb glisten.

Frosty soldiers stand on dueling hills
mounds of snow balls their hands to fill,
soon to hear the squeals and laughter.

Hot chocolate smells at kitchen door
graham cracker marshmallow smores,
trusty sled will have to wait until tomorrow.

Mary H. Clark
Modesto, CA

The Road Is Dark

The road is dark, I dare not stray from
Off the path of evil forged its snaky
Hands through which I slip—like Satan
Peers, from out the pit a city stretches
Towards the sky! As clear as glass looks
To the eye of Fear and Flame we dread that
Opens up when two worlds collide: Event
Horizon (view so dim) upon a distant star
Within an inch of matter, black and deep!
That keeps the light from inside creeping
Antimatter all that shines and pulls into
Itself a world that shallow lies beneath
His tomb—sealed brick by brick—a distant
Fog upon my cheek? Then pale with maggots
Riddled does my skin absorb, like Judas as
He kissed our Lord and all we could be now
Is swathed in leper's rags and wet with sores.
Ancient Baalzebub so fair, flies with compound
Eyes that stare! Through each leaf shrouds this
Road so black I do not dare to swerve or stray—
We're almost there! The woods are dense and dark
And deep, to either side I must not creep; her
Rusty, bucket-dwelling babe awaits my touch. The
Salty brine, the fetters 'round its tiny wrists
Entwined—in terror I awake from this dream…

Justin D. Weaver
Crossville, TN

I am from a small town in the country. Most of my life I have suffered from a variety of debilitating psychiatric afflictions and always used poetry as an uncompromising and emotionally empowering escape into personal nirvana of sorts, my very own garden of secrets burgeoning behind an impenetrable locked gate. However, I never believed in myself or my talent and I was always afraid to make that first step—the poem you have read is actually my first, and I have been writing less than a year. I believe that I possess something unique; I hope you'll agree.

Feelings

I often feel left out,
As my mind fills with doubt.
Does he really like me?
I don't know.
As my feelings for him start to grow,
I wonder if his has started to flow.
Feeling denial in my mind,
But remembering his words so sweet and kind.
Remembering the greatness of the past,
Waiting for that spell of love to cast.
I don't know what to feel anymore,
I'm about to head out the door.
He acts so different when we are alone,
Seeming as if he were a clone.
Trying to consider if I'm falling in love,
The butterflies in my stomach flutter their wings like a dove.
Gazing into his beautiful blue eyes,
My mind keeps telling my heart lies.
I don't know what I should be feeling,
I guess I will just keep on dreaming.
Dreaming of the perfect man,
I often ask myself if I can.
Do I deserve it?
I will find out in the future to come,
But for now my heart will continue to be dumb.

Michaella L. Croston
Waynesburg, OH

Hope

Hope
Its the last thing to go
once you have lost hope
you have lost everything
And when you think all is lost
when all desire is dire,
bleak,
diminished,
There is always hope.

Ryan P. McGlynn
Bloomington, IN

My Reason

Written for My Three Children

I first saw you I had tears of joy
I first held you I could never let go
You are my strength and every reason to live for
You made me someone and so much more
I cherish and adore every moment we will have together
You teach how to be a mother
Our bond so strong and never-ending
Nobody or nothing will ever come between us
You're my pride and joy
You're my reason to live my life on and on
The love we have will always go on
I love you Andy, Shaylee, and Sarina

April M. Rice
Davenport, WA

Lurk of Violence

Violence: a part of our daily lives
Violence: a heart of evil at night
Violence: lurking through the pitch dark light
Trying to spread worldwide
Violence, teenage gangs, politics, marriages are all good examples
and causes of violence
Chasing me down to the path of wrong
Looking at me in the eye
Straight up at me with a bland stare
Hate rate in the form of violence
Blinking down at me with silence
The sun rises the moon sets but violence never leaves
The souls of evil come and tap me with loneliness.
Friends, families, and many souls carrying violence
Why say....schools these days are not any better at all?
Robberies seen every day, everywhere
Please stop! I've seen it all
"Help, help," shout the innocent
As miserable as violence is the severity lasts in pain
Why? Why? This nonsense
Why not peace?
The blazing sun shines
The cold white snow falls
Hoping at least today we'll find a way out of this trap of routine
"Help!" yells the bright beautiful day
"The lives of our people are destroyed," cry the gods
The painful truth, violence is hurtful, and brutal
Illegal should violence be
No one should use violence

Allen John
Missouri City, MO

I am in 8th grade, and I enjoy reading and writing poetry. I am blessed with a good family. The thought that inspired me to write this piece of poetry was the incident that occurred last year when a teenager killed his mother because she was insisting that he study. Violence is all around and it is each individual's responsibility to make a difference. I am grateful for this great honor of giving me a chance to express my emotions. I accept this as a challenge to light the "light of peace in this world," with my few words.

Silent Magnolias

The way you bloom
The way your radiance emits such
a glorious aura
A power whose influence takes shape in
human form, and worships your beauty
The crimson fluid dripping from the tip of a sword isn't worth an
    ounce of your flesh
Glamorous women mask their lips with scarlet pigments hoping that
    one day people will aspire their elegance
Venus herself, as pulchritude as the bluest of seas, sheds the
    loneliest tear at your allure
lustful for your beauty, envious of your charm...
Winter's arrival ends my suffering, timidness of the image of you
Solemn magnolias reprieve and come to pass
as the petals of Rose, wither with bereavement with snow's ubiquity

Robert T. Walton
Moreno Valley, CA

I am a student currently attending high school. I want to thank everyone who supported me and believed in my poetry. I enjoy reading and writing all types of poetry. However I wasn't sure I could make it as a poet. I owe my inspiration to my family and friends, and I would like to give a special thanks to my grandmother, Pearl Rayfield. She never gave up on me even when I couldn't see the light in myself.

Disgrace

I love you, even though you smack my face.
I just lower my head in disgrace.
You show your love by blackening my eye.
You hit me more if I cry.

You put me in my place with your big, strong fist
Or when you grab my arm and break my wrist.
I think you are truly amused
By the way that I'm abused.

I feel ashamed with my arm in a cast.
And when my face is all bruised and smashed.
You call it love. I call it sad.
Either way, I'm the one who hurts so bad.

I want to leave you
But I can't get away.
Because of the kids,
I just stay.

Holly R. Reynolds
Mt. Sterling, KY

We Think We Are

Shadow of doubt
Within; without
Around about; in day light
from all directions
I see them about
Our mirror image
A face we cannot escape
An embryo from another time
Another space
Reflections copying us
Shadows on the sand
Mirror image of us
Always together
But forever apart
Are they the true reality
We think we are
While we look at them
Are they looking at me
To believe in what we are
Is what we think we see
We are what we think
Just you; like me
We think we are
What we see
A shadow reality
Can this be

Jeanne H. Laurin-Crawford
Anchorage, AK

There are shadows of all kinds in our life. Some in the mind tucked away in a closet but they are still there. Our doubts, shadows continuously follow a mirror image like a ghost in the mind, they disappear and reappear. There are many shadows according to light. They circle us and we are never alone. We are in another realm, a reality visiting our space and time. They walk up walls depending how far away or close we are. To them, they can be child's best friend to the end.

Don't

Though you were hoping for a break
From the madness of your life,
Your whole future would you take?

Don't make this big mistake,
Put down the sharpened knife,
Though you were hoping for a break

Your mind, so awake,
Your plan, so precise,
Your whole future would you take?

Your whole self you can remake,
Don't pay the final price,
Though you were hoping for a break.

Us all you would forsake,
With not one piece of advice?
Your whole future would you take?

I hope that soon your sense will wake,
And stop internal strife.
Though you were hoping for a break,
Your whole future would you take?

Morgan T. Coyle
Cary, NC

Apology

I never meant to grow old.
To lose my youth.
My intentions in life have always been true.
I have grown old and found myself not being free.
My movements have impaired me.
I have placed my life in your hands.
I'll never ask for more than required.
I must apologize for having the incurable disease.
If I could write a perfect destination it would have to be when I was
two years old.
My destination was handed to me,when I received polio.
My destination in life may have taken on another struggle, trying to
find common ground.
My apology to those who felt I was a burden to lift or wash me.
The blindness and ignorance that these people have, make me ask,
When will they give me an apology?

Lisa Rodi-Estrada
Cranston, RI

I am the third daughter to Mr. James and Virginai Rodi of Crunston Rhode Island. I have one son who is married with two boys. I am a local chef and enjoy writing, photography, gardening, and drawing. I also support ASPCA and defenders of wildlife. My poem was inspired by my father who has Polio. He recently broke his leg and had to spend time in rehabilitation for therapy. During his stay my father expressed great emotions. My father has always been independent. He supported his family by working every day and not taking any public assistance. My father has inspired me to live life to the fullest.

The Extent of It!

The moment dictated.
Chest flexed with open spaces
New vacancies in audition's row
A response in transition.
Not one that encompassed
Fast and furious medals of honor
Lining up for its disclosure.
Thoughts pursued what was
Coming down,
The bare essentials
Of its filled decision.
Steering on to its current reality
Spinning a nature, which drew upon
The interest of a nearsightedness reality.

Patricia H. Fritsche
Indianapolis, IN

Siren's Pleasure

She steals in
from under the locked closet door
drowning the room with promises
in a vapor of last night's perfume and rum.

She wakes you from someone else's dream
like a movie you've seen too many times in your sleep;
the button stuck on your life's remote.

You see the white flag in her eyes and know it's a lie.

Her self-absorbed mission disregards
the reality of failure with whimsical surprise.

You see the tangle of strings in her hands
and wait for a commanding tug.

Like a Flying Dutchman
you search for answers wandering in a fog
as your heart and soul and logic disconnect.

You see the storm rise from the calm and there are no life boats.

She rains venom in the face of trust
and sends you blind in waves so distant you doubt…
You doubt…You doubt…You…

Frances Ann Leo
Rochester, NY

Beauty Takes No Holiday

Another glorious day for me
Strolling along the edge of the sea
Footsteps seem to follow me—

Sights and sounds emanate the air
Seems to be coming from everywhere
The surf entwined with the breeze
Sing in sweet harmony—

Outstretched canvas appears to cover from land to sea
Revealing abstracts in pastels familiar to me—
Figures and loungers appear everywhere
Umbrellas scattered here and there
Apparently Monet and Picasso arrived before me—

Sun's rays shadow the beach—
Spilling crystals at my feet

Bellow blue drapes the sky
Setting the stage beginning the show—

A symphony of motion in dance
As rainbow of birds fill air
Acrobats and divers appear everywhere—

Fragrance of sea's perfumed scent—
Adheres to me—

An enveloped feeling of warm embraces
Sails in on the breeze—

Never do I walk alone for a vision
Of beauty is alongside of me—

Life's never-ending—
For there will always be—

The sun, sand and the sea.

Joan Lippe
Daytona Beach, FL

The World Is a Tangled Web

Judgemental minds,
putting on labels
Drawing lines,
cutting people out.
The World is a Tangled Web

Conceited peers,
thinking they're much greater
Causing tears
without even knowing.
The World is a Tangled Web

A backstabbing friend,
who you thought was true
But then it came to an end
because of their actions.
The World is a Tangled Web

People committing crime,
thinking life would suddenly get better
A waste of their time,
which will bring guilt later.
The World is a Tangled Web

Yes, people can change their ways,
start with yourself, build up from there.
Make it better for our kids' days,
so it is not as bad as this.
Will the World Ever Untangle its Web?

Rebecca E. Berlin
Southfield, MI

Sitting in Your Favorite Chair

I saw you when I walked into the door
sitting in your favorite chair
your feet propped up in comfort
and a book upon the floor
you glanced my way and smiled warmly
while I just stood and stared
you beckoned for me to join you
and as I crossed the room I noticed
how frail and wan you looked
I bent down and placed a kiss upon your cheek
and hugged you dear
it was good to see you after so many years
we sat and talked of all that had once been
of family and friends and places you wanted to see
you told me things I never knew and helped me
along the way as I grew
you showed me how to dress
how to make friends and how to truly impress
you taught me right from wrong
and through your wisdom I became strong
when I left I had learned new a respect for you
and though I didn't know it was the last time we would be together
the moments we had will last forever
I traveled to the places you wanted to go
I brought back pictures for us to share
and when I heard you passed away
I tucked those pictures in a box to be taken out on a rainy day
and remember what you meant to me and how much I cared
Sometimes I wonder, if I walk into that door
will I see you sitting in your favorite chair
with your feet propped up in comfort
and a book upon the floor?

Dawn M. Bertagnolli
Costa Mesa, CA

318

In My Dreams

Where'd you go?
Why'd you leave?
The only place I see you is in my dreams,
Close enough to feel too far away to touch,
The images I see appear so real and I want them so much.
I wish they were, so I would be able to feel and hear the noise of
your actual voice.
You leaving this earth wasn't a personal choice.
One day I'll see you again, but until then I'll continue to visit you friend,
Because my love for you will never end.
And until then, please continue to send the dreams that you seldom do,
Just know every night when I lay my head down I think of you.

Angel R. Hernandez-Sargent
Richland, WA

Crying

Crying is a natural gift as a way to relieve.
Crying is a natural medication as a way to heal.
Crying is a secret not to keep but to share.
Crying is a tip you should keep as tension releases in your tears.
Crying is a God-handed tool to appease us when overwhelmed.
Crying is a key to unlocking overloaded pressure.
Crying is a way to re-open a door in your heart.
Crying is not weakness but the strength you have to recover from setbacks.
Crying is not bad as a moderate one does well to your soul.

(Let's *cry* when we feel the need and let's be grateful to have this gift.)

Muyleang Kaing
Santa Ana, CA

319

To Prejudge Something

To form a sudden hate for me
to cringe
disgust
and apathy
To judge a book
by its cover
to think that I deserve to suffer
To hate me
'cause of who
I am
To my self-esteem
continuously
ram
To say things about me
behind my back
When I raise my white flag
you still want to attack
To bash on things
that make me smile
to say things
that are crude and vile
To ruin out of jealousy
to cut me down
like I'm a tree
To prejudge something
with all your might
To overwhelm me with
your spite.

Brianna R. Brooks
Providence, RI

The Wild

I looked up at the northern sky in wondrous awe,
and saw a shiny ribbon running so wild, like a shiny star
Now I am shoved in a crate
Not able to escape
I am on a boat
That barely even floats
The crate gets carried off the boat
Into something that looks like a fur coat
The men called it snow it glowed
I pull the slay all day as the snow violently flowed
With my frozen toes
Then they hit me on my flank with a hose
My friend is Curly he is another dog
But another dog name spits attacked him like a hog
The owners name is Hal
They do not treat the dogs like a pal
I do not like Hal he hurts me in my heart
I do not get to go to a warm park
I do not even get a lunch
I wish I had a carrot to munch
Now that John Thornton dies
I have nowhere to go but the wild for a while but the wild

Liver Cole
Venice, FL

Stopping This Feeling

Arrow to the heart,
Dagger to the soul
Trying to find peace inside this hallow hole

Gun to the head
Or knife across the throat
Trying to stop the pain before it swallows me whole

I hate this feeling
Like nothing's inside
It's stronger than the pain
And it just won't slide

Without much time,
I have to think fast
Take a life away,
Or just try my best?

Lorenna J. Malotte
Lincoln, MO

Brother?

Brother's breast a bloodied mass,
And mass a masked shame.
Pray hard pray low the blood still flows,
And life ebbs like the tide.
Brother! Brother! Stay and shun the moon!
Brother! Brother! Live and curse the wind!
Too late, too late, a blood bathed beach.
A gore gushed grave of faded youth.
Too late! Too late! A cry too late!
Too late. And far too early!
Hide the moon! Stop the sun!
Curse the night and blow hard the horn!
The wall is fallen! So why are you?
Curses! Curses! Brother? Curses!

Carley J. Fisher
Millville, WV

Strand of Spaghetti

As I see the spaghetti, I am absolutely lost in it.
Each little strand that is so barely heard—
Screaming for help—praying that someone will notice them.
Not just someone—someone special,
Someone like the Parmesan cheese—
Who they are dying to be with forever.
But the little strand of spaghetti is so tiny, so minuscule
That no one as great as the Parmesan cheese would ever fall for it.

Or the ripe strawberry,
It will never be good enough to meet the person they most admire—
The warm, rich, creamy chocolate,
No, never—not once.

Or even someone as humongous as the giraffe,
They will never get that one, perfect piece of grass
They dream about.

Neither will someone as scary as the bee—
Ever find that tall, purple lavender they wish for.
And the lavender doesn't even know this bee exists.

In this case, I am the strand of spaghetti, the ripe strawberry,
The humongous giraffe, and even the scary bee.
I am calling for you
But am lost behind the many others surrounding me.

Everyone should know that they have a follower
Waiting endlessly for them.
Whether it be for love, admiration, or even curiosity,
There will always be that one strand of spaghetti.

Monica L. Mishra
White Plains, NY

A Young Angel

A young, beautiful angel contains with a grace and dazzling smile
like a lovely, radiant violet flower displays in the green flourish
spring

I am a young angel
passionate like a hot fire covered by the dark night

I am a young angel
submerged in my own feeling like a boat sunk down in the deep ocean

I am a young angel
invisible like a rosebud waiting to be bloomed in the spring

What have I done wrong?
Why do you break my heart into two?
Does needle of guilt trouble your conscious that you deeply wounded
my heart?

Oh! you do not love me so I weep until tears from my eyes become
like raindrops falling from the sky and the sweat turns into blood that
drips to pillow

My mind lets go of many things like the blessing of life and the gift
of love and hope because my heart still belongs to him and can't let
go of him.

Look! God, the charming angel is crying in mourning for the loss of
her loved one.

Why does the pretty angel have to be a heartbreaker? God endows
her with a good mind and charming beauty. Does she know that the
magic of love is the precious thing to have on Earth and there are
many more to come?

Hanh N. Chau
San Jose, CA

My Reverie

Again and again you let me down
And yet I'm here
I fell to the ground
You have broken my fall
Then pushed me back down
In and out of your arms
You can't seem to decide
And I am stuck
For your gravity won't let me up
You smile, I melt
You talk, I freeze
You stole my heart
And didn't replace it with yours
I'm barely breathing
You give me hope
Then take it back
Time ticks on
I'm cold in this world
Alone without you
Stupid fairytales and happy endings
For forever and always
My dreams live on
No matter how hard I fall
Or how long I'm down
You can't take from me
My reverie

Ashley L. Gatchell
Oakdale, PA

Halls of Dung

Prancing or walking lifeless beings surround
holding signals to an ear transmitting hopeless nothings
Monkey see, monkey do,
For how true, a revealing revelation.
I can smell you the vermin stretched out on the floor laughing.
High heels scuff and mark, leftover remains of the night before.
Ale, whiskey, 2 or 3 shots, harbors, swirling in your head.
Marked with temptation, eyes of sorrowful angst.
My breath echoes over to you.
A glimpse of ponder?
Smells of chalk dust, markings on the bathroom wall.
Now clinched, whispers overflow like a wound.
I follow, willing, waiting.
Dirty crusted over, sweet moisten bliss.
Let's flop down together and disappear.

Gary C. Robertson
Chico, CA

To a Person

I have a secret for you,
One that can be understood only by you
I've kept it for so long
To you is where it belongs;
I don't know how to tell you this
So I shall just spit it out:
I hate you.
There, I said it.
It wasn't hard
Now was it?
Let me explain before you say anything;
Talking will loosen up my pain
My love was a game I played with you
Did you really think I loved you?
I couldn't help but pretend
I knew you didn't want this friendship to end
But I am done feeling sorry for you.
I am going to let you go.
Farewell, my friend—
I hope you enjoyed my show.
Why I kept this a secret,
I don't know.
Now that it's finally out,
I hope you understand
That I hate you
And that's how it will be.

Abou Ibrahim-Biangoro
Santa Clara, CA

Hate and Tolerance

Why is it
Hate
   Often prohibits
     The brain from working
     Turning common sense
     Into anger
       Which in time
         May become revenge
         Cold
           And frequently
           Deathly violent
Why is it
   There are always those
   Hate
     Will control
     Will cajole
       Into destructive action
Why is it
Hate
   Seems much stronger
     Than tolerance
       And its end result
       Peace
Why is it so much easier
   To hate
   Why is it so hard
     To learn
     Toleration

John E. Taylor
Fort Wayne, IN

Conflictingly Different

Always there, but always silent.
Never there, yet so loud.
A constant smile that's never sincere.
Inconsistent tears that are always real.
Sweet lies that drip no truth.
Words of hate that bleed so true.
Tenderness that isn't what it seems, no gentleness has ever been seen.
Rage that is thought of as an act of kindness, it's what I deserved.
Pain, that is a pleasure. His privilege.
Joy, that is forbidden. My anguish.
Love is not meant to exist. It never did.
Yet and still somehow a relationship was built.
I don't know how I came to love you.
Or how *we* even came to be, 'cause we are in no way the same.
We are conflictingly different.
I must find a way to leave.
Or you…and your twisted ways will be the end of me.

Tori S. Greene
Heartland, TX

Love

I love him but I cannot show it,
want him but he cannot know it,
You don't know what you mean to me,
you don't have a clue,
you can't tell by looking at me what
I feel for you I'm scared of everything.
I'm scared of what I feel, of what I say,
of who I am,
but most of all I'm scared of walking out of this room and
never feeling the rest of my life the way I feel when I'm with you

Love is like a mountain hard to climb,
but once you get over that mountain it's a beautiful journey......

Jyssica N. Harris
Kissimmee, FL

Missing You...My Love!

Somewhere in the dark, lonely night
I feel my heart's restless fight
Curdling up all blood inside
Bubbling up your dreams in sight
Calms me down, my mind rests light

Things I see remind me of us
Of all those times we spent joyous
When over rocks, streams they flow
Comes to mind your smile, its glow

Lovely paths of green both sides
Yet I give them lonely sighs
Gazing at stars alone at night
I wish I held you close and tight

In coffee shop, as pairs share love
Next to me, I miss my dove
Love of you gives peace of mind
A welcome lease from daily grind

I miss those roving eyes in car
Now shortest places seem so far
My dusty car has tales it tells
Of past sweet and dreamy spells

Fly to me, I can't just wait,
Run to me, don't make it late,
In my chest drown all head's weight,
Fill up my heart's empty plight

Joey V. Louis
Land O Lakes, FL

September 11th Remembrance

Nine years have passed and people come together to remember.
They say it was the day we suffered the most. The day we will never forget.
I say it was the day we were made weak. We spend all our time
defending other countries from tragedies like this, but when it comes
to defending ourselves we hide behind our flag.
We are Americans! We are the land of the free and home of the brave.
We've spent our entire history defending that title and now we hide!
I once read on the back of an American flag package that you take
down your flag at night and bring it in from the rain and storm to
keep it safe. But what does that really mean? What does that say for
us? Whenever things get rough, if it gets a little dark
or a little wet to hide and keep ourselves safe?
I don't know about you, but I was taught that being an American meant
you can get through anything no matter how rough it gets, or cold
and dark or even a little wet. I believe that as Americans we should
be standing in the rain with our flag held high letting the whole
world know who we are and where we come from.
Letting them know that we will fight anyone who stands in our way.
I believe we should always honor and remember the loved ones
who lost their lives in the September 11th tragedy.
It was a loss I will never begin to understand and their lives can
never be replaced.
I also believe that this tragedy could have been prevented.
They had the information stating that something was going to happen
and yet they did nothing to prevent it.
We take it seriously when a child has a hit list at school or comes to
school with guns and who is blamed? The parents! Well I believe
that the people of America are the children and the government is the
parents. So now who is to blame?
Letting some less minded people who are jealous of what we have
and what we stand for bring us down.
We don't teach our children to let people make them feel less than
what they are because they are from a different race or creed.
We teach them to stand and fight for their rights and to never let anyone
make them feel weak or vulnerable.
I am an American and will never let anyone tell me that being who I
am is not good enough.
And my flag, which is the American flag, will stand through harsh winds
and torrential rains, through tornadoes and hurricanes,
flying high not hiding where it is safe.
For it is the American flag and like me it is strong and ready for anything.
For nothing and no one can keep me from being who I am and what I
stand for. I know where I come from! I hope you feel the same.

Elizabeth D. Fogg
Fitchburg, MA

A Dreary Day

As the sun peeks through the clouds on a Dreary day,
All the flowers has began has began to bloom on a lovely day in June.
The birds all singing in the trees, the sweet scent you can smell from
the summery breeze,
The birds fly down to take a bite as your presence surrounds them,
they begin to fly way out of sight.

On a Dreary Day in June the horses all running through the fields,
You can hear a soft voice whisper through the clouds saying, peace
be still.
On a Dreary Day in June the chickens and the roosters all in the barn,
Singing cockadoodle doo and having some fun too.

The roses are red and the violets are blue,
There's no one else around but just me and you,
Sitting under the sycamore tree of hope and love
Just counting the clouds in the sky above.

On a Dreary Day in June as I sat on the hill and watched the smoke
Come out of the chimney from the stove in the house,
Mother in the kitchen cooking some food,
While under the table sat Henry the old middle-aged mouse,
Eating on a piece of cheese, and running back and forth
Through a hole in the crack of the house.

Now it's the end of the day, the sun is almost down.
The Dreary Day is almost gone, the sounds of the birds has stopped.
The chickens are asleep in their nests all tucked away,
Waiting 'til morning comes to begin a brand new day.
Whew! I'm tired now, this has been my Dreary Day,
But thank God everything worked out okay on this Dreary Day.

Sandra A. Shelton
Birmingham, AL

I chose this poem out of hundreds of poems I've written. I also write short stories
on various topics; none of my short stories have been published. This poem was
written in 1998. I thank God for the gift he has instilled in me to write. I've been
writing since 1980. Mrs. Shirley Whitson would always encourage me to carry a
pad and pen at all times because so many things would come in my mind I had to
write it down. I've been married to William Shelton, Jr. for twenty-nine years and
we have three children named Angela, Cornelious, and Johnny Jr.

Say What You Need to Say

Say what you need to say
Even when the tears threaten to fall
Even when it might break down that wall
That you have been building since that day
So go ahead, say what you need to say

There is always someone ready to listen
Who won't care if you start to ramble
Just let it all out, don't hold it in
Open your baggage and start unpacking
There is always someone who can share your burden

It's as easy as that
Except when it's not
But if you want to talk
Just come my way
'Cause I'll let you say what you need to say

Kaitlyn R. Blunt
Essex Junction, VT

Ten Thousand Raindrops

Somewhere, a beetle lands on a window sill
Tangled in a web a wasp lays still.
The sun sets for a couple in bed
While it rises on a road untread.

Four snowflakes melt on a rabbit's fur
Storm clouds moving, love-deter.
Ten thousand raindrops grace the sky
Ten thousand people gone awry.

A horse confesses secrets to the wind
Through cavernous wires, thirteen computers compute and have sinned.
Miles of hills, a churning green sea
A snake hordes the secrets in the hollows of a tree.

From blue iris, tears gush and flow
Broken glass rests beneath the mistletoe.
Someone just now found a beetle to kill
The hope of this world murdered on a window sill.

Momo A. Gogo
Levittown, PA

spellbound

lost
in silent wonder
held fast by another's will
as she fills my mind to overflowing
feather soft her kisses blowing
and thus for one brief interlude
in the stillness of my solitude
lost
in silent wonder
so very deep that i may drown
lost am i and furthermore
i pray i'm never found

Robert A. Metcalf
Rochester, NH

Memories of Love

Painter
I met a man so long ago
Who painted
Many pretty things
He spoke through them
Like poetry
He even painted one of me
As time went on
I came to see
How much this man
Has meant to me

Leticia Aguilera
Salem, OR

Three Perfect Words

Perfect only speaks three words,
Of what the heart needs been heard,
The spoken grace of love that stands,
Ideal love as they hold hands.

Speak a time of good that passed,
Remember summer love that lasts,
Be in thought in time and heart,
Don't be afraid of life's new starts.

Think of them with love and grace,
The perfect times were set in place,
Of where that love had grown to be,
Forever together is what you see.

So think a moment that can't be gone,
Three perfect words that sing a song,
Look real close and you will see,
Three perfect words are, "You and me."

Kristopher J. Kamps
Tallmadge, OH

The Giggling Shed

Locks shatter, panes clatter as the whispering wind visits the door.

The aroma simmers as if it was fire crawling over the dusty floor.

My senses change as zippy as flipping channels with a result of a
    damp musty smell,
as if the minute little shed was under a spell, so strong it comforts
    your fierce souls
like a mother's heart relaxes a baby, like a mother's heart relaxes a
    baby.

Though yes I *can* hear, this may appear queer, that shed giggling
    rapidly
and now I am sure for it opens its door to let me join in, to let me
    join in!

Holly V. Astley-Sparke
Weston, MA

Hello, I am currently a fourth grader and writing is one of my favorite hobbies. Writing poetry helps me express my feelings in words that form my inner heart. I have a family of five and my grandmother is very inspiring in her poetic style. My family has always kept my confidence high. Looking out my window with zooming thoughts of my backyard shed inspired me greatly and my imagination made me believe the shed was alive like in "The Giggling Shed."

Phone Lines

She met me in the end, to send us to the beginning.
A life of ruins spent in lies.
A cover up of misfortunes she brought to my eyes.
Sudden dreams of hopes took me away.
A vessel to carry on waves of forgiving love.
Awoken to a smile and a song.
A beauty written in glass, shattered into reality.
A day, a month, a year.
Intertwined by sound brought in by the wind.
I'll meet you in the phone lines.
A new escape into simplicity.
Memories roll in with the waves.
Left with a yearning of past promises, awaiting chances for the unknown.
The sun reflecting misery to shame.
Pictures in the sand reminding me of her, my home.
Rescue me...rescue me...
Make me whole once more.
Past sins please forgive them, take my hand.
Hold on to me.
Please say it's all the same.

Samantha N. Miller
Yuba City, CA

Lonely Soul

The beautiful wildflower
basks in the warm sunlight each day
It reaches up to the sky
to catch the warmth of the sun with grace
The flower sits alone at the edge of a wood
The sad, sad breeze
rustles through its leaves
singing a depressed song
Clouds come rolling in,
the angry storm starts
but the clouds soon part
leaving tears running down the flower's leaves
Lonely in the woods once more
Lonely in the woods once more

Emily H. Sedlak
Northbrook, IL

I am a eleven years old and I am a 5th grader living in Illinois. Ever since I was a little girl I've always loved to write, especially poetry. I entered this contest to challenge myself. My hobbies include tennis, squash, violin, and writing.

The Story of a Restless Insomniac

Beating, beating
cannot sleep
maybe it's time to count some sheep
one...two...three...and four
this has sort of become a bore
this wondering mind
my insomnia has become my bind

Beating, beating
I cannot sleep!
I feel a little tickle on my feet.
Yuck, uhck...get away!
Why must these feathers be uh-fray?

Beating, beating—this time a little
   too fast—
What is this feeling which is so vast?
Thump-thump, thump-thump
I'm pretty sure now it's my heart that goes bump, bump, bump.

Beating, beating
   stop ignoring it...
this feeling obviously seems to fit
Sitting, wondering, is it so?
Well it must be
or I wouldn't be sitting here writing this poem.

Breanna M. Soliz
San Marcos, CA

In the Midst of Everything

I knew you from somewhere long ago,
I think in some hidden place in the atoms of
The brightest stars,
From the beginnings of everything,
There we were floating together,
One bright star in all of the darkness,
burning forever,
Time bursts forward,
Life blooming,
Stars moving,
But there in the very beginning
Of everything,
We were tied together
By the molecules
Of some long forgotten star,
Destined forever
To remain together
As one
In the midst of everything.

Kelsey A. Swanson
Hudson, NC

Our Valentine's Day

I wish you a happy Valentine's Day
Do you remember our last one?
I am head over heals in love
I can feel our love bond

I love you so much
Now we celebrate our first kiss
Our God gave us many blisses
To protect our true love

Come enjoy this
Valentine's Day
Notice of our love
Anniversary

Build our life happier
With it
Honest and fidelity
To love together

Celebrating our first Valentine's Day
Honor our second Valentine's Day
Respect our third Valentine's Day
Love strongly our Valentine's Day

Darling, please love me tender
Love me with your gracious heart
I can't live without you
I will surely die if you leave me

Thu V. Tran
Winooski, VT

Most Valuable Player

Faster, faster! Don't stop now,
Catch the ball and juke him out.
Reach the end-zone, take a bow,
Hear that crowd scream and shout.

Look at your girl in the stands,
Cheering at her very best.
You smile as she waves her hands,
Stay focused now, no time to rest.

Thirty seconds left to play,
It's up to you to win the game.
The quarterback looks your way,
The fans begin to chant your name.

Run the ball down the field,
One last time is all you need.
Your teammates act as your shield,
And you speed up to gain the lead.

As each yard line passes by,
You realize that your job is done.
Raise your arms to the sky,
Because of you, your team has won.

Sarah R. Gilbert
Costa Mesa, CA

How I Think God Sees Me

One thing I know for sure
is that God's love is the ultimate cure.
No matter what he sees me do
I know his love will guide me through.
There are no secrets between God and me,
I know he knows my destiny.
And no matter how stubborn I may be,
I know he's always there for me.
To pick me up and hold me tight
and scold me when the time is right.
I feel like a bird just spreading my wings
and learning so many different things
like no matter how bad my life may get,
you can bet something good will come out of it yet.
I may not see it right away, but when I do I will say,
"Thank you father for this day.
Your unconditional love is more than words can say.
You made me laugh, you saw me cry,
and now I know the reason why:
to make me strong, to make me grow,
to make me the person I now know.
Not the person of yesterday, but the person of today.
Yesterday's gone and today is here,
and what tomorrow brings are God's set of wings
to wrap around me and hold me tight
and tell me its going to be alright."

Claudia M. Clark
Bakersfield, CA

I was born in southern California. I am married, and we have four children. What inspired me to right this poem? My soul needed cleansing. I was recovering from an abusive relationship. With baby steps and the ever supportive mom and dad I was able to keep moving forward. God's constant reassurance that I would find faith, love, and peace I thought that only existed in fairy tales. If you have a heart that is healing, for whatever reason, I hope you find some healing comfort reading this poem.

Free Heart

A heart yet to be free from burdens is as a day is to eternity
To yearn, as a wanting child that suckles at a mother's breast
A heart to be free from pain
scarce as a bountiful rain in the desert
Can we not seek that which we may never grasp
to go toward the essence of a pure heart
burden free, pain free,
We can but life, as cruel as it is
seems to thrust itself upon us
Not wanting all it offers, not expecting all it gives
With all that is piercing our spirits
it's no wonder the heart shows itself vulnerable
Looking towards that one day
when pain shall cease
a free heart and pure heart shall at last be free
free from all things that hold us from all we can achieve

Ronald S. Mager
Munising, MI

Emotional Waves

A Beach
sandy, warm, soft
happiness, excitement
water lapping
it seems peaceful
until
Testing the waters
meeting with the first wave
emotions run high
it was everything you thought it would be
lustful thinking
the wave is gone
the second wave
the thoughts the same
sky darkens
more waves come
eating away at the beach
eating away at you
exhausted, overwhelmed
each wave seems the same
you pray
please, one be different
sweep me to safety
battered, bruised
hoping the storm passes soon

Heather N. Miller
Cincinnati, OH

typical teenagers

you always want what you can't have
and you always cry even when others laugh.

you ask a question even when the answer is clear
and you have to listen to things you don't want to hear.

if the point of leaving...is not to return
then why do you go back...to where your heart is at home?

you may dream in color, maybe white and black
it isn't that which matters, it is the sight, the fact.

if there is contest of who is winning and who is to lose
who will be the lucky one? it is you who will choose?

so if it is any help, the guide to being a teen
just live on...live the dream.

never stop fighting until the time you are dying
and live without regrets to pay...tomorrow is a new day.

Amber C. Whitt
Burnsville, NC

The Winds of Change

The winds of change are sweeping me past,
parts of my future have opened at last.

I am not able to break free, you see;
these winds are hurling me towards my destiny.

I ride along blindly, not knowing just when
these winds will ever let me down again.

My hair's flying wildly 'round 'bout my eyes,
I grasp at thin air and hold onto blue skies.

I look for an opening, a chance to break free,
while parts of my life race crazily by me.

I jump and land running, not knowing just where
in the world I'll end up, I say a quick prayer:

"Just help me this once!" I scream up to the man,
He just laughs and winks like this was *His* plan,

"Calm down, dear one," he says, as the wild winds descend.

"Now then, shall we start this all over again?"

Terry A. McGarry
Cherokee, IA

Follow You

I can follow your footsteps
In the freshly fallen snow
wandering slowly behind
you know where to go
But the forest to the left of us
will always catch my eye
Did you see it there?
I swore I saw something I should try

Mae A. Lewis
Leander, TX

Stare

The people stare
Like we shouldn't be there
They see black and white
Dark and light
Equality it's there but together they tear
Bald heads in the night they tell young kids to fight
But should we?
Keep it pure or add the cream
Are we all on a different team?
We all have hair, skin, eyes, and a head
But the one thing we don't share
Makes us so different
That people can stare

James S. Husband
Jacksonville, FL

My First Love K2

We met when I was five
I had on a button up with my shirt tucked inside
There you were Brown with a white line and a Nike sign
I knew I wasn't blind you had to be mine
The sun rays beamed on you and all you did was shine

The grass put you in disguise but I was hypnotized.
Some criticized that one day when it was over I would sit in corners
    and cry
That isn't fact that's a life my love till I die.
My euphoria my high tucked under the peck as I glide
Dodged one to my side victory food hotdogs and fries

Offense or defense it didn't matter to me
But when 93 is on the field he's all he can be
Just like his Uncle Moe on the TV
Who played for Philly ironically in the year 1993

God was on my side the reason I strived
I needed first prize it made me feel so alive
The rules were abided and the tools were inside.
It's a shame I didn't make weight I was only over 5
But having family behind my back I had so much pride.

I don't mislead or misguide I can play everything give me a try
Standing 4-foot-9 athlete at his prime I can assault with my helmet
    but its not a crime
White cleats shining like dimes perfect target his spine this game is mine
Just one shoe lace at a time if I could rewind
Just one last time I would celebrate with a peace symbol in the end
    zone sign

11 on 11 the angels had an open view from the skies it was
    Showtime my first love and I
With a win here I would shed a tear because my first love gets rid of fear.
You shaped me into the young man that I am today
 Kiss on your laces as I would never forget the day
 My first love you opened the way

Alphonzo White
Landover, MD

Man in Tree

There once was a man who lived in a tree.
So high up he could not see the ground.
Then one day in his high tree from the ground there came a sound.
So loud it rocked the tree from the top right down to the ground.
Then his world started to fall and he tumbled to the ground.
He yelled "Watch out below, for I am heading down."
As he hit the ground he saw there were people gazing all around.
There were spaces in all their faces as they stood around on the ground.
Scared, he turned to see a face as black as coal
with eyes that would eat your soul.
Then it opened its mouth as he fell to his knees.
No sound was found anywhere around.
He saw all the trees now hit the ground.
The air disappeared and he felt he was drowned.
Light faded away turning all leaves from green to brown.
His tears fell from his face to the ground.
All he could see now was that black face.
With eyes so red you could see them from space,
As he became dead in the face of the ground.
Then there was a loud streak of light and sound.
With his last breath he saw a white horse.
As he fell to the ground the light struck those eyes.
And the darkness let out a nasty sound of pain from the light.
As those dreadful eyes close you feel warmth all around.
Then your eyes open with a great insight.
You're in your bedroom with your cross on the wall.
And there's no one around to be found, none at all.

Shane A. Fritz
Caldwell, OH

As a child, I spent a lot of time in the hospital. With pen and paper, I grew to love
poetry and writing. I love the poetry of Edgar Allan Poe.

353

I Had a Dream

I woke up one morning and was scared out of my mind.
So many questions I wish to ask, behind my face is where they lie.
I never knew it would happen to me,
so I went around to go find. My heart ached of a horrible pain
I never felt before,
my tears cried beyond my tears for my eyes were so very sore.
My brain ached of lamentation from this miserable sensation.
I just couldn't wait any longer I could not be patient.
Every one had I was the only one,
I couldn't wait for this chastisement to be over,
I don't know what I've done.
Everyone was in a passionate fold to love and to hold.
Thinking of me having the same, the idea couldn't be sold.
This indomitable dream hit me in a malicious kind of way,
I was so flabbergasted I could not say.
This feeling was so esoteric I could not believe
that a passionate feeling like this it was me to deceive.
I got on my hands and knees and talked to my father from the sun,
Audaciously he pointed his finger down and said it cannot be done!
Everyone was wrapped in a passion and overflowed by doves.
The manifestation of the dream I had was I could not be loved.

Edna Henry
Orlando, FL

Teflon Poisoning

Every time I look at the clock, I realize I have unmatched socks.
Perfect I was thinking as she just kept drinking and drinking.
Her socks don't match as well, I said kiss me and I won't tell.
A hot tub filled with cold water, I couldn't have wanted any other.
It was my 26th Valentine's-Birthday and I thought I was all alone.
She read my mind then left the next morning, my mind was blown.
I wonder what she was thinking, and if she kept on drinking.
I got home from work, I couldn't find her anywhere; she was sinking.
I searched everywhere, I couldn't possibly imagine where she would be.
And then finally I found her sleeping restfully, sweetest I've ever seen.

The car is running out of gas and it's cold outside.
I will bring her somewhere warm, to the ocean, fall in love by the tides.
She wants to marry me she says, she promises she will be my bride.
I will love her forever and I know our love will never die.
But I need her to stop drinking because she needs to stay alive.

Pamela L. Binette
Beebe Plain, VT

Road to Recovery

Since I was eleven, I have had a hard way,
I used that as my excuse for the trouble I got in every day;
Always used my conditions as a crutch for things I'd done,
But I know that I was lying, I did them purely for fun.
All the disrespect, the hurt and damage I have caused
Could never be fixed, not ever, or at all.
I had an anger problem, and I would just bottle it all up,
and one day I exploded and I got put in lock-up.
Now, I am almost eighteen and I have honestly changed my ways;
I'm living a better life and having much better days.
My dream of changing the world has yet to come true,
but I have not given up and that I'll never do.
Poetry is all I have now, and that means so much to me,
I hope by this poem you can truly see.
My passion for writing is like a dog and a man,
I cannot do very much, but writing I know I can.
I give it my all and I do it a lot,
It comes from my heart, and this is my only shot
to prove to myself and others that I can be something someday;
I got to put my mind to it and not let anything get in my way.

Christina N. Hutcherson
Fairview, TN

Another Sad Song

Another sad song,
stop singing.
Another thing gone wrong.
Melodies ringing,
In these ears of mine.
all I hear
Is one line,
Over and over.
Please make it stop.
It's tearing me apart!
Pain, sorrow,
It's all I feel.
Please make it not be real.
Make this pain go away.
I don't want to be alone,
So please stay.
I cry as the song
plays over and over in my head.
I hope I'll soon be dead.

Lucy J. Rudman
Milton, NH

My Life Is Like a Flower

My life is like a flower, it makes it strength to grow, to get stronger.
It lives and gets pretty, stems are pealing off and it gets old.
Dig it in and dig it out.
Every day it goes on with the same patterns over and over!
My life is like a flower,
that every day there's a new story but always the old moves.
You live in the pain but get stronger the next day.
My life is like a flower, it needs water to live,
but you cry and cry and no one wiping them away.
It grows and grows,
but the pain gets harder and harder and it's hard to stop them.
My life is like a flower,
when it comes to Valentine's Day you take a flower and peal out the petals and say,
"He loves me, he loves me not." The pain lives and then the pain dies!
Water dripping, but the sun comes out and dries them away.
You live longer and then the smile will come out!
But my life is like a flower, but can you say?

Jesenia Cabreja
Reading, PA

Forgiveness

Word is a weapon that targets the soul,
It can make you carry heaviness on the chest
It will make you cry, without tears
Or...
It will make you feel like a butterfly,
And smell like the best flower that God created

Word is weapon that targets the soul
And then comes back to you,
Because your mind is the nest of your soul.
If somebody gives you heaviness
Let the word sleep in your mind....

Mind can break roots,
Mind can put mountains together.
Choose to feel free,
Forgiveness for others is your power to fly
High in sky and overlook the soul and mind.

Word is the weapon, forgiveness is the power.

Nancy Vee
Graford, TX

The Lost Girl

Lost in her ways, goin' through a phase.
Looks in the mirror and gets lost in a daze,
trying to search for herself;
the person she never knew,
the boyfriend she has is stuck to her like glue.
Blue is how she feels when she's all alone,
when her boyfriend comes over she's laid down like a phone;
she's gone, in her own zone.
Blown away by her man's love,
she swears that God sent him from above,
flown in by a white dove.
He's gone, she's blue, he flew away from her home,
She's blown away by the weed she just blew.
If only someone knew, how she felt when she is blue.
If only she knew what is true about who she is.
But she's lost in herself, and that's just the way it is.
She's the lost girl, and that's just the way it is.

Malcolm J. Hayes
Vero Beach, FL

God, Can You Hear Me?

Can you hear me?
I'm falling
Faster than I could ever imagine
They tell me about you
On the deepest days they tell me I need you
I come crawling to you
I fall. Fall more than ever
I'm lost. I need you
I need your love
I want you to be with me
I need you in me
I want you to have plans for me
Falling, you catch me
You bring me to the light
You love me. You live in me
I'm ready to move
I'm ready to be more like you
Hold on. Don't let go
Teach me. Show me
I'm ready
God can you hear me?

Taylor E. Israel
Victoria, MN

Guardian Angel

You have fought this battle and now you've won
You share your time with God's only son
You'll watch over us with a close watchful eye
It's just so hard having to say goodbye
The time we spent with you is something we all would enjoy
That is something no one could ever destroy
Even though your passing brings with it pain
Your spirit in our hearts will forever remain

David J. Daniels
Waco, TX

A Blank Sheet of Paper

A Blank Sheet of Paper
All dressed in white
Not even a drop of ink splashed on it
Nothing to say
Nothing to write
Makes for one long night
So here lies the paper
All plain and white
No one needs it
No one wants it
Nothing to say
Nothing to write
Poor blank sheet of paper all snow white

Debra L. Bender
Medford, WI

The Vibes I'm Receiving

He asked me my name and from then it was history.
I could tell he'd be important the moment I heard him speak.
I was cautious the minute I felt my heart skip a beat.
I could tell the mark he engraved would remain there permanently.
I was approached, unaware, off guard, and unexpectedly.
I was surely and swiftly swept off my feet.
I could tell by his timidity he was intimidated by me.
I could tell by his hesitance he was eager to touch me.
I knew by his persistence, he was anxious to know me.
I was convinced by his patience that time meant everything.
I was eager myself to see where it would lead.
I found comfort in his strength and confidence in his sincerity.
I knew I found a friend from the way he made me laugh.
I knew there was a chance he'd be my better half.
I began to worry when it was him I was constantly thinking of.
I knew there was a possibility that I would fall in love.
I could see he was afraid, the way he'd shy away.
And when he'd see me coming, he'd walk the other way.
Still, I could tell he wished to hold me 'til I was out of breath.
And pour out his love to me 'til there was nothing left.
I knew that circumstances prevented us to know.
I knew he understood I had to let him go.
And even though it was no longer him I was constantly thinking of,
I could tell there was a possibility that we were already in love.

Lanae B. Johnson
District Heights, MD

My poem was simply inspired by a good friend of mine who liked me as more than
a friend. Although the feeling was mutual, I was already in a relationship and could
not act upon them. Thank you J.A.T. for inspiring my poem.

The Fallen

I look down the long unending road,
Why must it continue?
Why must this pain never end?
I'm alone. Why should I keep going?
I have nothing to live for.

My heart yearns for a companion,
When I am alone there is nothing to see,
Tears stream down my face,
Like this unending road,
Won't it just *end*.

I no longer walk among you,
I am more
Untouchable,
A picture of anger and pain,
I will never walk among you.

You may be next to me,
But I don't feel you,
Don't feel the heat I need to satisfy me.
I am stone,
Rock hard, stone.

I am deadly,
A killer,
Your worst nightmare,
Your greatest enemy,
The things that go bump in the night.

I am the fallen.

Mia S. Jones
Ladera Ranch, CA

To a Girl I Know

This is to a girl that I know,
a girl who hides in a darkened shadow,
the one that cares about everyone,
but doesn't want to let it show.

This is to a girl that always cries,
a girl that always runs and hides,
the one that wants to live,
but inside she fights and feels to die.

This is to a girl that everyone's afraid of,
a girl that everyone tries to run away from.
The one who's misunderstood and not heard of,
but she tries to speak her mind.

This is to a girl that I know,
a girl who doesn't like to feel.
The one that wants to heal,
but she doesn't know how.

And this is to a girl that I used to know,
I knew her like the back of my hand.
She changed so people could understand,
but she realized no one ever will.

And this is to me.
The one that wants the world to change,
but wound up changing for the world,
the one that tries to hide,
the one that always cries.
The one that I knew like the back of my hand,
but I've changed.

So this is to a girl that I know.
But I'll never let it show.

Emma L. Melendrez
Wayland, NY

Purr

She is perfectly perfect,
Licking her paws,
Stretching her claws,
Careful to keep them quite clean.

She is royally regal,
Prim and haughty,
A tiny bit naughty,
Sitting as if she's a queen.

She is daringly daring,
Tiny tiptoeing,
Where is she going?
Secret cat business unseen.

Sweetly alluring,
A kitten's light kiss,
Absolute bliss,
Peacefully sleeping. Serene.

Wendy L. Schmidt
Appleton, WI

Danielle

When I was six, you were born
Sweet and cuddly, you, I totally adored.
While you were little, we stayed great pals,
Then you were six and got really loud.
I was a teenager, filled with anger and hate,
I took it out on you, and you forgave.

I got pregnant and had to leave home.
The hardest part was leaving you alone.
I never told you then, but you were my best friend.
Your letters every week got me through.
I never would have made it without you.

It was your turn to be a teenager.
And again, I was filled with hurt and anger.
You always bore the brunt of my issues,
Then forgave me, and loved me too.

I have put you through a lot,
And still you forgave and forgot
I don't deserve a sister like you,
with a heart so steadfast and true.

You manage to love me, no matter what,
And have never returned the crap you got.
Now that we are grown-ups and friends,
I want you to know, that I will love you,
'Til the end.

Kristy L. Smith
Mauk, GA

False Deception

I question whether it's real or a flaw in my perception
And subliminally, the world
Slips into oblivion,
Suddenly my equilibrium
And grasp on reality
Are fused together eternally and sucked
Into a black hole; shaken unto vertigo.
Every thought that enters morphs and becomes
A new reality.
Limbo entombs me,
I'd like to fall back down to Earth
And steady my step.
I'd be happy to be sane
Where reality will never leave my locked grasp
And nothing holds the key.
The blue sky surrounding,
The earth beneath my feet,
My head never in the clouds,
But everything around me, lies?

Sophia P. Andrianakos
Centennial, CO

My Heart and Soul

Our love is written in stone
We will never be alone
My love for you is endless
I've always made this known
for it's not just my soul
but my heart you own

William R. Rackley
Sturgis, MI

I am married to a beautiful woman named Rebecca and we have eight children, seven girls and one boy. It was our twelfth anniversary and I tried to think of something different. My first thought was to write a poem, then I thought I would engrave it on stone which turned into a big rock. That's where the beginning of the poem came from, "Our love is written in stone." I dedicate this poem to the love of my life, Rebecca Rackley!

My Belly Bubbles

My belly bubbles, buttons testing durability,
pants bulging to the very outskirts of their limit.
Zippers leaving imprints on my flesh,
like footsteps hunger has left behind, little red indents
I stare at, rubbing my finger slowly across them.
Diets digested, denied.
A funeral dirge sounding,
with a line of dessert delectables marching its wake.
Giggle, rumble, snap.
The pants collapse. An army of fat cells band together arm,
pushing against skin, throwing rolling punches.
Their attacks leave purple and pink lightning bolts
'cross hip and thighs.
Hanging guts salute chocolate goo dribbling down
double chins.
The glory of abundance. All hail fat.

Esther A. Albrecht
Decatur, GA

Black and White Creativity

Lost in the sunset, wind blowing softly,
the sky a slight pink.
Enlightened by a cemetery where many lay to rest,
a church where many are blessed.
Sinners and cheats, Christians and Catholics,
what's the difference between these two worlds?
One's less chaotic than the other?
The other is more loving and sweet
than a junkie's life on the street.
Forgive sins and accept the fact that time is not able
to turn back. Re-live memories,
and see the mirror beyond the beauty of reflection,
see inside, past the skin, in the heart,
in the emotion that feels right.
The world is closing in, gasping for air, receiving smoke.
Looking into the sunset, its bright gaze a distraction, a daze.
The sun disappears and nothing is left to see,
but the pale white moon, reflecting in Amber waves.

Amber D. Martinez
Provo, UT

Blues Over Coffee

She stares a porthole through her coffee cup,
a tunnel of escape.

Anvil thoughts on peacock feathers,
her sadness curdles the milk.

Possible scenarios
puff up like soggy Cheerios.
None, a disinfectant for the truth.

Memories in a stack of Polaroids,
she deals and shuffles like a game.

Trip, trap, truculent.
A tussle of turmoil
tented to tainted trust.

The reality spike,
an embedded tick,
the stigma...she is incomplete.

A new cup of coffee,
a new set of directions,
an arduous effort en route.

Mark Rinn
Dearborn Heights, MI

The Blood Runs

The blood runs
could it be because of a knife or a gun
the blood oozes
regardless of the end
out loud speaks the clues
igniting a short fuse
on the inside there's every excuse
with every tear of flesh, there's a deep sigh of breath
and now I find myself enmeshed
My eyes are swollen dry
in every way I find a way to deny
built to defy, also supplied with an amplified alibi
no longer will I sing myself to sleep with a lullaby
all along, I now know it is my time to testify
no one has heard enough of me and yet no one can see
once I used to be carefree
Now the scars are well hidden
on my wrists and knees

Melissa M. Morse
Phoenix, NY

Son of God

There is a man named Jesus, he was born out of a necessity to quell man's evil. He was born to teach, and heal the sick, to build our faith, and to teach us to pray to one God.

Jesus took unto himself all of the man's sins, and all the bad things that were inbred within.

He had a unwavering faith that man can change from his wicked ways. From all the great things he achieved in his mortal life. We crucified his body but never his life. His spirit dwells in all of us, he walks and talks with us every day, but do we listen?

His voice resonates even in a soft whisper. Between right and wrong, we know the way, we just have to pray for forgiveness. Each of us has done things we're ashamed of or not proud of. But if man or woman won't believe that people can change, Jesus will.

Because we all fall short of the glory of God. These words I speak are not biblically written but biblically inspired by the man we call the Son of God.

Jesse McClure
Chicago, IL

The Man in the Moon Has a Lover (a Riddle)

The Man in the Moon has a lover
She lingers aloof, yet astride
And like a good husband he hovers
To see that she shines by his side
The luminous glow, they've discovered
Is where halos from Heaven collide
The Man in the Moon has a lover
Forever the groom and his bride

Angela M. Shaw
Wellington, FL

Drinking and Driving

Every time you put that bottle to your lips,
I think of what might happen,
but I don't want to fight with you,
and you have no idea how I feel about you,
but it's not a big deal,
only that I could lose you,
but you refuse to listen to what I say and you drive on those roads
like it's a speedway.
At any second something could happen.
It frightens me,
the thought of losing you.
You just don't understand things like this are never planned.

Maygan A. Hays
Trenton, FL

Open Your Eyes

Open your eyes love, open your eyes for me.
Let me know you made it to Heaven peacefully.
I loved you right from the start and it kills me now that we must part.
Open your eyes love, open your eyes for me.
Show me that you understand that for so long I've loved you.
I loved the way you looked at me and said our love was meant to be.
Even when people said our love was wrong I knew the truth because
our hearts beat to the rhythm of the same song.
Open your eyes love, open your eyes for me.
Please love, just breathe another breath.
Promise me that you will always be with me even after death.
Open your eyes love, open your eyes for me.
Promise me you'll keep me in your sight.
Just promise me everything will be alright.

Beth A. Dillinger
Morristown, IN

Why Me?

Why did I have to go through this pain?
Because of you I live in vein
I cannot handle this anymore
I cannot help but fall to the floor
I need to feel safe again
I do not need this pain again
I wish to come back
But I do not want the attack
I want to be everything
But without you, I cannot be anything
These wounds may never heal
No one knows that this pain is real
You cut in too deep
I want to enter an endless sleep
I am in so much fear
I am almost in tears
I feel like a ghost
Because I want you the most
I am alive
But I don't know how long I can survive
I want to be wrapped in your arms
I just do not want the harm
I remember when we used to kiss
But that's not what I miss

Sierra A. Glover
Las Vegas, NV

People

People come in all shapes, colors, and sizes.
They can be fat or skinny, tall or small,
People can be happy mad or sad,
But we would all be alright if someone shut off the lights.

John R. Walker
Sioux Falls, SD

Life Is Here . . . Death Is Coming

The seed planted months ago.
Twig coming up through the snow.
Years go by; tree is grown.
Something someone should never own.
Time flies for this young pine.
It's the caterpillar's time to dine.
Snow is falling yet again.
Logger is coming, 6 foot 10".
Here he comes with his axe.
Don't look now sharp as tacks.
He chops it down; takes it to town.
It's set up in a lot. Now it is bought.
People take it home. Decorate it with cones.
It is now a dead Christmas tree.

Skye J. Franklin
Santa Fe, NM

Just a Tree

This paper I hold
I wonder about
If its branches were twisted
And turned all throughout

If its leaves were as green
As the clover below
And how did it look
When covered with snow?

I wonder and wonder
And wonder out loud
"Would it like to stand tall
Once again if allowed?"

And if it were
Could it reach to the sky?
Would it reach to the moon
If it did try?

What color was it
Before all this white?
And if it had known
Would it put up a fight?

If it had seen
What its future would be
Would it still choose
To be just a tree?

Tessa L. Rosenberg
Arnold, MO

The Edge of Ruin

I stand on the edge of ruin.
One step away from destruction.
Like a ship without a sail I sit there,
waiting for the currents to take me where they will.
Waiting, fearing, hoping, praying that I will
drift where I want to go. Then weaving, sewing,
stitching, piecing together a sail. A sail of memories,
experiences, hopes and dreams. Now I sail like a bird,
like a cloud. Flying across the waves, not falling into troughs,
or getting stuck in doldrums, but skimming across the crests, faster
and faster, into the light, the dawn and the end. Yet it is not
the end, but the beginning.

Noah A. Cloak
Northfield, MN

Temperance, a Virtue

Once in a land given to divinely original statutes there had been
Temperance as a virtue, praise for composing oneself.

To refrain does not entail restraint, character is defined by your
Freedom to choose your acts; What you have chosen to do.

As we but know a man by his expressions, ideas, what he says;
Here, place your intentions, ingrain your self in your words.

Withhold from tongue unfit notions and base phrases, keep clean
your subjects,
Mold with your mouth a frame, for you to fixate your mind.

Josef D. Windau
Shorewood, WI

Blue Firmament

The blue firmament so high above
Embraces the ground in act of love,
And wraps its misty arms about
Ending the land's eternal drought;
It calls a meeting with the clouds,
Deciding matters with voices loud,
And majestic powers, all unfurled,
Determine the fate of Earth and world.

Stefanie R. Milovic
New Fairfield, CT

The written word is like a part of me, a part of my world. It's the lone cloud wandering sky, the leaf dancing towards ground, the unique beauty that intertwines all our lives together. In poetry, everything is my inspiration. This poem is for everyone that helped me aim high, reach far and become the proficient writer I am today! Especially, I would like to dedicate my poem to Mrs. Economou, the best writing teacher anyone could ever ask for! She's been a major source of my encouragement all year and has illuminated many aspects of my life today.

For It Was Never Love

It was never love
It is these four words that drive into my back like a thousand daggers
As I sit in my own puddle of blood and drown in my tears of sweet
    sorrow
Ah sorrow, I kissed the tender lips of sorrow
And stared into the very face of pain
At first only with the numbing coldness of your sweet loss
Take it, I pleaded
As I offered nothing more but my broken heart to him
Take it, and rid me of his forgetful nothings
I know it was never love
And with my last cries it was then that sorrow kissed my lips once
    more
And pain snatched my heart
Left with nothing. Empty. Lost. Alone.
My body, robbed of the only thing I had left to offer him.
And yet for what price did he pay for my pain?
This ruthless beast was not worth my suffering was it?
I think not.
And yet now my soul rots away
Broken and deteriorating of all life it once possessed
For it was never love…

Meradith L. Brown
Ellensburg, WA

Where Were You?

Where were you when the little girl cried out to you
Tryin' to ask for help without asking but you
Never took her serious and you thought she was
Crying wolf for the hell of it?

Where were you when you heard about the scars
On the little girl's arms, even though she understands
You have a life of your own but still you went on with
Life as if nothing happened?

Where were you when the little girl wrote her problems
In a way you would understand but yet you continued
To ignore her as if she was a stranger to you?

Where were you when the little girl spent lonely nights
Crying thinking she was nothing and feeling as if she
Wasn't worth the ground we walk on?

Where were you when other people called the little
Girl crazy because she wanted to end her life but never
Thought to stop and try to understand or to ask why?

Where were you when the little girl got fed up with
Life and tried to choke herself to death, even though she lived?
Why do we value someone's life when they're dead?
Life should be valued when he/she is alive and tell your
Loved ones you and appreciate them each and every day.

Martha A. Edmond
Brentwood, CA

O' Mother Ocean

O' Mother Ocean, can you forgive,
All those who pollute you, on land we live,
I am sorry your waters are dirty from us,
I know we have lost your valuable trust.
Please do not blame every one of mankind,
We all aren't a part of this hideous crime.
O' Mother Ocean, I love you, I do,
Your bountiful spirit,
natural waters so blue.
The infinite appearance you cast on this place
Will always affect the entire human race.
It's a disgrace all waste that is thrown
With carelessness into your fabulous home.
We cannot clone you once you are dead,
So please stay alive and hear what I've said.
Bad thoughts I do dread but I'll defend your glory,
Even if I have to tell the whole world this story,
With faith I hope you know that these words are true.
O' Mother Ocean, we love you, we do.

Donato D. Di Carlo
Jacksonville, FL

In 2001, I wrote several poems including this poem. Once I finished the poem I realized how moving it was to me. Growing up surfing the beaches of Jacksonville, Florida, I developed a love for the ocean at a very young age. I gave a copy of it to my mom for Mother's Day one year and now she has it framed in the dining room. My ultimate plan is to add several more verses to it in order to turn it into a song.

An Old Man's Valentine

It looks like love is in the air
Valentine's Day he hopes to share
Card is written in shaky hand writing
For wine and dinner he is inviting

Up there someone pulls the string
Birds on high begin to sing
Cupid's arrow comes from above
To the heart of the one you love

A gift to her he does present
He does this with real intent
It is a rose there is a hush
This even makes her blush

A sultry look a hidden wink
He does not know what to think
Playing footsie under the table
Oh my goodness he hopes he's able

This all leads to a night of bliss
Starting off with a loving kiss
Looking deeply into her eyes
She knows he is thinking of her thighs

Love is now in the air
Valentines they do share
All is not what it seems
As he now wakes up from his dreams

Blair Thomson
Sellersville, PA

Goin' Down Beignet Street

Café Du Monde with their sweet beignets from the sweet sugar to the chewy caves inside the bread.

As I take a bite a burst of jazz goes in my mouth.

The sugar as the saxophone, and the bread as the trombone.

They all come together and make a great sound.

After jazz it goes to screaming fans singing, "Who dat?!" to the grand finale of a swallow and a smile.

Trent R. Hernandez
Mandeville, LA

I am ten years old and I am in fourth grade. I am the youngest of three boys. My two older brothers are Garrett who is twenty-four and Travis who is nineteen. I am already an uncle to a nine-month-old little boy named Travis Jr. I take karate and I am a blue belt. I like to play football, ride my bike, and skateboard with friends. We did a book assignment about Louisiana. My inspiration for writing this poem was that I like jazz, the Saints are my favorite football team, and Café Du Monde is a wonderful place to be. My teacher, Ms. Willis, taught me similes which I used in my poem.

why?

this life—
i live free—untroubled
hopeful.
in mine presence, kin
and enemy fall.
why?
the life they live—
haunted, desecrated, deceived—
tortured.
existing only by
nonexistence
so much hatred.
so much fear—love
why?
why not be true?
why not set free?
burdens of such
are our holds.
in short i realize...
for i am perished—
i am the deceased.
this is why
i live in hope freedom
to lose nothing evermore

Luke C. Brown
Wichita, KS

Today, Yesterday, and Tomorrow

In loving memory of SFC Makishma C. Wood
6/14/1980–9/18/2010

Tomorrow is here, today has become yesterday…

I feel what I felt yesterday, I see what I saw yesterday.
Tomorrow I will feel like I did today and yesterday…

I will feel and see that day for the rest of my life.
There are no longer yesterdays, today or tomorrows…

My life stopped on that day.
The promise of tomorrows left me that morning.
Never will I feel your love again…

This is what my life now is, from now till my tomorrows are gone.
That love that we could feel like no other today,
but wanted to feel it again tomorrow is now gone forever,
now that my best friend is no longer here from yesterday…

I close my eyes and see you, like I saw you yesterday.
Your smile, your voice and beauty will never be found tomorrow.
I see you in your kids, your smile and gestures today…

I would trade all my yesterdays and tomorrows for that one night
with you.
I miss you, Makisha, with everything I have inside me for all my
tomorrows…

Gene O. Gallegos
Rio Rancho, NM

Dear Diary

Look at me and what do you see?
Shame and pain, thunder and rain?
Look at me and what do you see?
Depression, loneliness, low self-esteem?
Or just some one in need?
Look at me and how do you feel?
The need to run, the need to squeal?
You see me walking down the street and
you feel your heart sink in one fast beat.
You don't want to see me, you don't want to hear me,
so you sit down and fear me.
But I'm here, your worst nightmare.
Nobody likes me, nobody wants me around.
I feel like a piece of dirt lying on the ground.
I feel sick to the bone just lying at home. I am all alone.
Look at me and who do you see? This is because I smoke weed.
I threw my life away, when someone came to say,
"Do you want some cocaine?"

Amber R. Prete
Wolcott, CT

Our Duties

The future is the key,
So be all you can be
To live happily,
Despite adversity

We need to trust,
Respect life enough,
Live by rules; not unjust,
Love each other truly,
Never be unruly

Help your fellow man
Develop a good plan
To prosper and succeed,
No matter what his creed,
Despite all the greed

It is essential to be expediential
In this cold hard world,
Although we may swirl,
We must find our place
To save the human race!

Lillian R. Bradley
Louisville, KY

The Lover's Woe

Day by day you call my name.
Night by night we remain the same.
We sigh so deep,
For the lovers weep
And come to me in misery.

Love to love we float along,
Heartbreak to heartbreak we remain strong.
You say you know
The lover's woe,
Yet you come to me,
In vain,
And bring only misery
And pain.

Alexa R. Kaufman
Independence, MO

forgive me

you hate me because i left. i left and showed my soul and all the scars it holds. now you won't forgive me, so i cry with everything i have. i wish that you'd come back, come back and save me. and i'm alone i feel the world so cold because you left me.

now all i need is time, time to clear my mind, forget about the past. but you won't forgive me, so i die a little more inside. my soul fades and it's fading fast, so i try, try to understand why this hurts me.

i know you hear it all every time i call and i say love fix me. can you feel the tears? they're running on like years. i know you hear me, so pick up on the phone and let this love come home and please forgive me.

i know it was so hard, the tearing of our hearts, the bleeding and the pain. would you forgive me? give me another chance; i swear i'll change my plans just please, please love me.

Lindsey R. Woodring
Fattyeville, PA

A Very Special Day

Two lives become one
on this very special day.
I promise to be there for you,
and in my heart is where you stay.
For you bring hope to me
with the little things you say.
I walk not in front of or behind you,
but beside you all the way.
For you are my best friend,
and my love will never stray.
You make me smile
when my skies are gray.
You are the one
who makes me merry and gay
and devote my life to you
on our wedding day.

Barbara G. Lejeune
Hot Springs, AR

Repent

Many times I feel the pain
the tears that fall.
How could I
commit this sin
against the Lord of all?
I know how much He loves me
and how I love Him so,
but still I turn away from Him
and wallow in my guilt.
But then I turn and see my Lord
and turn from all my sins.
I run into his loving arms
serving only Him.

Timothy D. Lewis
Spring City, TN

A Man Did Stand Up

Away from England we must break,
Into a war for a freedom they cannot take.
Onto Lexington then Concord our soldiers go,
For the outcome of each we did not know.
Regardless of when this war will end,
To lose England our so-called friend.
Near the end we seem to come,
Down south we go and will not run.
Since seventy-six we yearned for this,
Unlike the Tories we will not miss.

Allison Goldsmith
Frankfort, IL

One More

*Dedicated to all parents that have lost a child
due to drug and alcohol addiction.*

One more tender kiss as I hold you close and tight,
you're just a tiny baby don't ever leave my sight.
One more gift at Christmas as I open up my last,
why does it have to end, it comes and goes so fast.
One more tender kiss as I hold you close and tight,
you're just a tiny baby don't ever leave my sight.
One more day of camping why can't you see the thrill?
I haven't even got to see what is over that next hill.
One more tender kiss as I hold you close and tight,
you're just a tiny baby don't ever leave my sight.
One more dog that's all I need to complete me don't you see?
Or maybe if I had a love that would love me just for me.
If only I had the perfect car or one more day of rest,
I'd be your child and go to school and finally pass the test.
One more tender kiss as I hold you close and tight,
you're just a tiny baby don't ever leave my sight.
I found the thing that makes me feel complete in every way,
all I need is just one more to make it through the day.
Now all you do is sit and cry 'cause one more day is done,
and now I know I should have lived and forever been your son.
One more tender kiss as I hold you close and tight,
you're just a tiny baby, why did you ever leave my sight?

Please help save our children

Patti Ludlow
Mapleton, UT

Caged Despair

I am Drowning.
Bubbling and Gasping for air.
Choking on the past and present.
Reaching out to grab anything to hold me above
this pool of tears but everything I grab
shatters and breaks.
I fall all the way back down.
Plummeting back into the Pool of Death.
the Pool of Sorrow.
The Pool of My Own Tears shed from the very eyes
that you love.
And I start crying again.
And the pool just keeps getting bigger and bigger
Until it's a lake
Or an ocean.
My sadness, my sorrow
put into one small droplet of salty liquid descending innocently
down my face.
Then cascading like a waterfall.
Thoughts become Reality.
Reality becomes Thoughts.
I cannot stop these salty tears of sorrow
From dripping down my sad crying face.
No one can.
No one ever can.
Memories in every tear.
Crying away the memories.
The good and the bad sliding down my once smiling face.
Yet now, it is no longer smiling.
It is no longer smiling, but screaming in pain.
The same face that cries even now.
Still.
Forever.
I am Drowning.

Sean Ciminello
Dartmouth, MA

The Day of the Haunted Mansion

"Drip drip"
The soul replied
Sitting in the haunted mansion
"Tonight we fight
For freedom and exposition"
The soul got up and ran to the door
And with a cry you could see more
More and more souls did come
Marching in the millions or some
They ran to the mansion and stuck together like gum
"Run, run" the soul did say till the day is done
The souls ran and ran till the sun did rise
Then they ran to their crypts with their aching cries
The sun rose and softened eyes
People glanced around with fear
And questions began on the pier
The little girl standing there
With her golden brown hair
Said finally to the people on the pier
"They came last night like every year
While I sit upon this pier
They came to destroy the town
until they saw the news going round
The town was good and nice
And the smell of spice
and took them from the rice
and they noticed
The town was nice, they found again
And celebrated good will to men
so they hide in there house
till the town is quiet like a mouse
They will creep and sneak out again
until the world comes to an end"
She left back to her house that day
Then instructed the souls to come back and play

Haley Hornung
Eldersburg, MD

Fearful Yet Full of Fear

Fear,
An ungodly gift to man
used to dilute one's motivation.
Fear,
Corrupts the mind
And makes some stray from destination.
Fear,

Known as wisdom of harm
But Wielded by enemies Fear becomes a manipulative trade and a
deadlier charm.
Fear,
parent of Murder, stress and jealousy,
Its cousins called
Hatred, betrayal and infidelity.
Fear,
A curse known to us since the tree of knowledge
The more we learn, we fear; this urge is both fueled and pacified in
college.
Fear,
We cannot live without it.
Praised and celebrated is bravery
But all brave men have known a great deal about it.
To conquer fear one has to be royally skilled,
Great Goals are needed and equally willed.
Humanity Will Fear! The feeling is drilled,
The Brave ones will be feared, and the feared will be killed.

Marc Pocorni
New York, NY

Every Day

Every day is a good day when spent with you
Every day is the first day of the rest of our lives
Every day is made for you and me
Every day is made to be shared with you and me
Every day is made of memories shared by us for us
The memories we make today will not have to be on film to be
    remembered
To be remembered right, do right to be remembered for
To be worth the memories of tomorrow make the memories today
    that will last
Everyday memories can last long after you're gone
Your physical being will die but your memories will live on
Make your presents pleasant and so will your absence

Larry Daley
Wappingers Falls, NY

Bound

Bound by the laughter
Bound by the tears
Bound by joy
Bound by fears
Bound by the love we sometimes don't show
Bound by hate over time we've let grow
Bound by bad choices together we've made
Bound by the prices we've all dearly paid
Bound by the memories, some good, some bad
Bound by emotions, some happy, some sad
Bound by harsh words we'll forever regret
Bound by soft whispers we won't soon forget
Bound by two precious girls and one brave little guy
Bound are we all 'til we've all said "Good-Bye"

Shawna L. Churchwell
Whichita Falls, TX

Index of Poets

CPSIA information can be obtained at www.ICGtesting.com
Printed in the USA
270488BV00003B/3/P